the unbeatable Squirrel Girl

Like I'm the Only Squirrel in the World

the unbeat

COLLECTION EDITOR: **JENNIFER GRÜNWALD**
ASSISTANT EDITOR: **CAITLIN O'CONNELL**
ASSOCIATE MANAGING EDITOR: **KATERI WOODY**
EDITOR, SPECIAL PROJECTS: **MARK D. BEAZLEY**
VP PRODUCTION & SPECIAL PROJECTS: **JEFF YOUNGQUIST**
SVP PRINT, SALES & MARKETING: **DAVID GABRIEL**
BOOK DESIGNER: **JAY BOWEN**

EDITOR IN CHIEF: **AXEL ALONSO**
CHIEF CREATIVE OFFICER: **JOE QUESADA**
PUBLISHER: **DAN BUCKLEY**
EXECUTIVE PRODUCER: **ALAN FINE**

THE UNBEATABLE SQUIRREL GIRL VOL. 5: LIKE I'M THE ONLY SQUIRREL IN THE WORLD. Contains material originally published in magazine form as THE UNBEATABLE SQUIRREL GIRL #12-16. First printing 2017. ISBN# 978-1-302-90328-2. Published by MARVEL WORLDWIDE, INC., a subsidiary of MARVEL ENTERTAINMENT, LLC. OFFICE OF PUBLICATION: 135 West 50th Street, New York, NY 10020. Copyright © 2017 MARVEL No similarity between any of the names, characters, persons, and/or institutions in this magazine with those of any living or dead person or institution is intended, and any such similarity which may exist is purely coincidental. **Printed in Canada.** ALAN FINE, President, Marvel Entertainment; DAN BUCKLEY, President, TV, Publishing & Brand Management; JOE QUESADA, Chief Creative Officer; TOM BREVOORT, SVP of Publishing; DAVID BOGART, SVP of Business Affairs & Operations, Publishing & Partnership; C.B. CEBULSKI, VP of Brand Management & Development, Asia; DAVID GABRIEL, SVP of Sales & Marketing, Publishing; JEFF YOUNGQUIST, VP of Production & Special Projects; DAN CARR, Executive Director of Publishing Technology; ALEX MORALES, Director of Publishing Operations; SUSAN CRESPI, Production Manager; STAN LEE, Chairman Emeritus. For information regarding advertising in Marvel Comics or on Marvel.com, please contact Vit DeBellis, Integrated Sales Manager, at vdebellis@marvel.com. For Marvel subscription inquiries, please call 888-511-5480. **Manufactured between 1/27/2017 and 2/28/2017 by SOLISCO PRINTERS, SCOTT, QC, CANADA.**

10 9 8 7 6 5 4 3 2 1

Squirrel Girl

Ryan North
WRITER

Will Murray
WRITER, 15-YEAR-OLD
DOREEN SEQUENCE

Erica Henderson
ARTIST

Rico Renzi
COLOR ARTIST

Anthony Clark (#13),
Hannah Blumenreich (#13)
& **Michael Cho** (#15)
TRADING CARD ART

Zac Gorman
MEW'S DREAM
COMICS ART

Steve Ditko
DOREEN'S COSTUME
DRAWING ART

VC's Clayton Cowles
LETTERER

Erica Henderson
COVER ART

Charles Beacham
ASSISTANT EDITOR

Wil Moss
EDITOR

SPECIAL THANKS TO
CK RUSSELL

SQUIRREL GIRL CREATED BY **WILL MURRAY** & **STEVE DITKO**

Squirrel Girl *in a nutshell*

Squirrel Girl @unbeatablesg
Whew, I just had THE BEST NIGHT'S SLEEP OF ALL TIME. For some reason I feel like I could take on the world?

Squirrel Girl @unbeatablesg
Like, I woke up energized and jazzed, as if I really had just defeated a super villain and saved the world...IN MY SLEEP!! Felt great tbh

Squirrel Girl @unbeatablesg
But hah hah that's impossible so oh well

Spider-Man @aspidercan
@unbeatablesg actually there's a doctor strange bad guy named "nightmare" that you could've technically fought in your dreams!!!

Spider-Man @aspidercan
@unbeatablesg doc strange isn't on here though otherwise we could ask him

Squirrel Girl @unbeatablesg
@aspidercan A guy with a doctorate in strangeness doesn't hang out online here? WEIRD

Squirrel Girl @unbeatablesg
@aspidercan YOU'D THINK HE'D FIT RIGHT IN

Tony Stark @starkmantony ✓
@unbeatablesg Hey, how's that robot brain in a jar guy you patched up working out?

Squirrel Girl @unbeatablesg
@starkmantony Brain Drain? Great! Well on his way to becoming a real hero, actually! Still mega nihilistic but in a cool way

Squirrel Girl @unbeatablesg
@starkmantony We're going out on patrol together in a bit actually

Tony Stark @starkmantony ✓
@unbeatablesg Shouldn't you not mention when you're going out on patrol, so the criminal element won't know?

Squirrel Girl @unbeatablesg
@starkmantony good point my dude, one sec

Squirrel Girl @unbeatablesg
HELLO CRIMINALS, THIS IS JUST TO ANNOUNCE THAT I AM ON PATROL ALWAYS AND WILL DEFINITELY CATCH YOU DOING A CRIME, SO DON'T DO THEM

Spider-Man @aspidercan
@unbeatablesg holy crap can i use that

Squirrel Girl @unbeatablesg
@starkmantony Tony are you there I just had the best idea!! Tony tony tony

Tony Stark @starkmantony ✓
@unbeatablesg Hey.

Squirrel Girl @unbeatablesg
@starkmantony TONY. BRAINSTORM. What if you changed your name from "Tony Stark" to--HEAR ME OUT--..."Ira."

Tony Stark @starkmantony ✓
@unbeatablesg "Ira Stark"?

Squirrel Girl @unbeatablesg
@starkmantony IRA ONMANN.

Tony Stark @starkmantony ✓
@unbeatablesg oh my god

Squirrel Girl @unbeatablesg
@starkmantony Tony I'm going on vacation so I just wanted to give you something to remember me by

Squirrel Girl @unbeatablesg
@starkmantony just a little memento

Squirrel Girl @unbeatablesg
@starkmantony for my good friend

Squirrel Girl @unbeatablesg
@starkmantony ira onmann

search!

#braindrain

#canada

#nopowernoproblems

#maureengreen

So...since Brain Drain's on the case...

And since there are *literally hundreds* of other super heroes in NYC doing the exact same thing...

...y, Nancy, I know, it's just--with Chipmunk and Koi Boi using *their* week off to visit ...celona and the ruins of the underwater ...ngdom of New Atlantis, respectively, I worry!

Dude, *SO many* other heroes live here! Iron Man! Captain America! Two or three of the Spider-people, probably!

Yeah! *They got this.*

Oh my *gosh*, you guys. You've made your point. *Fine.*

I hereby acknowledge that there are *other super heroes* willing to keep everyone safe, and therefore, *yes*, we can take my mom up on her offer to have us come visit for a girls-only weekend.

...et's go ...Canada, ...ou guys.

Hooray!!

Nice.

So, uh--we're taking your New Avengers teleporter, right?

Oh we are *SO* taking the teleporter.

I've discovered the odds of a TSA agent finding a tail stuffed in your pants and saying "That's wonderful, I wish I had one too, please enjoy your flight for I have no further questions" are approximately *negative one billion percent??*

TSA agents freak out even if you wear *shoes* when you're not supposed to! They are clearly not yet woke enough for tails.

And so...

You got bug spray, Nancy?

Yep!

Sunglasses?

Yep.

Knitting needles?

And how.

Mew's staying with Biggs, and I even set up a vacation auto-responder for while we're gone.

Oh, that's a good idea! I should do that too.

Mine is set to reply to every single email I get with, *and I quote,* "haha lol no."

Hah!

I'm serious. I may never turn it off, actually.

I am finally free.

And I got new shades at a doll store for extremely stylish dolls! Are we ready? We're wasting prime lake time!

Last chance! Everyone's got everything they need? Teleporter's one-way, and it's gonna be a long bus ride back to NYC if we forget something.

So ready, Doreen!

Anything I forgot I will build out of sticks and leaves.

Okay, teleporter engaged!

KLIK

So assuming nothing goes *catastrophically wrong,* ha ha ha, the next thing you see will be--

VZZHHNNN

Other email autoresponses that have no possible downsides include "haha seriously?? tell me more!!", "interesting, let's follow up on this tomorrow!", and "who are you and how did you get this email?". Like I said, no possible downsides!!

Wait a second, *hold on.* Something's not right here...

No Fridge??

No light switches on the wall?!

Wood-burning stove.

Clock that needs to be wound?!

Really boring magazines that nevertheless seem to be well-read?

You guys. *You guys.*

There's no electricity here!!

That's what I was expecting. You said your mom got a cabin in the woods. What, you thought there'd be a hot tub?

It wouldn't have hurt! Nancy, I can't even get a *cell signal* out here. We're entirely off the grid!

It's perfect. We'll sit by the fire, wake up with the sun, and swim in a lake with nobody else in it.

Can't wait.

But... but...

but if i couldn't fight crime here i at least wanted to be able to fight it vicariously through tony stark's updates on social media

I had plans to "like" some criminal's tweets and then when they saw my "like" they'd Freak out and stop doing crimes, due to insecurity about my all-seeing social medic
I had *plans,* Nancy.

Brain Drain has trouble telling humans apart, but can remember their names with the efficiency of a robot man. In contrast, I can distinguish between *thousands* of people whose names I've long ago forgotten and now it's way way *way* too late to ask. Life is full of challenges, everyone!!

Well, we're here in the woods, middle of nowhere, nobody else on the lake. All our food is kept safe in containers so we don't attract bears or other scavengers. *And yet,* it keeps disappearing.

And I can't figure it out.

For example: I made twelve muffins before we all hiked out to the ridge this morning, and have the dirty pan to prove it. But there's only eleven in this container.

From a seal container? the lid *repla* afterwards

Mice?

Maybe a friend from town stopped by?

They would've ha pick the lock on door, eat the mu *reverse-*pick it o way out to lock behind them, *and* leave any footpr I don't think s

And it wasn't a squirrel either; the windows were closed.

So who was it?

Awww, Mom! It really, really is.

Well, that's the mystery I was hoping my super-daughter could solve for me! "The Mystery of the Missing Muffin." Just the thing to spice up a quiet trip to the cabin, huh?

All right!! I am *gonna* investigate this mystery, solve this friggin' crime, and never be bored again!!

Alternative titles for this case: "The Case of the Cupcake Caper," "Just Desserts," and "The Mysterious Muffin of Skellington Bay" (did you know: if a bay doesn't have a you can *probably* just name that bay??)

Canada:

Local squirrels don't report anyone coming or going for weeks, Doreen, except us. They--

...Huh??

Tippy? What do you see?

Not sure. Something small moved in the corner as I was coming in. Not a mouse.

What was it then?

I wanna say...pants? Red and/or green, possibly?

Pants.

Look, prey animal here. My vision's *so legit* I can see things out of the corner of my eye as clearly as if I was looking right at 'em.

And I'm telling you, I saw *something* in tiny pants slip through this crack.

Well, you're not tearing up the floor, Doreen. This is a rental.

No, that's fair...but there *is* another way. And it's arguably even *more* fun??

All right! Everyone out of the house!!

Most squirrels are red/green colorblind, which means they have trouble telling red and green apart. If you share this property too, then good news! You have at least one *squirrel super-power,* and that's more than most people can say!

Honestly: I'm not sure what I was expecting, but I feel confident in saying that "a tiny village beneath the floorboards" is the polar opposite of that.

Hey, are you a super hero?

EVEN WHEN I CANNOT SEE MY OWN POTENTIAL, I STILL STRUGGLE TO REALIZE IT

SO YES

10: STOP DOING CRIME 20: GO

Okay, super, great. My car's got a flat, and I was wondering if you could carry it and me back to Philly so I--

KRRTZT

Huh?

My fellow humans. Welcome to North Enigmerica.

I've spent the past decade placing my selves in your government, major industries, and military. We used a variety of false faces that are now no longer required, because today, we assume command of these resources.

Look, I know this is a shock, but I wouldn't be here announcing this stuff if it wasn't already settled. This is for your own protection.

For everyone's.

This is the beginning of a new age for humanity: an era of peace. An era without wars, without hate, without bigotry.

You tried, but you couldn't make it happen. But I could.

So, I just did. You're welcome.

10: STOP DOING CRIMES 20: GOTO 10

Great things are coming. While there are now armed guards entering major areas, if you treat them with respect, they'll do the same for you. Except for that, it's business as usual.

I'll let you know more as the situation warrants. Enigmo out.

Well, looks like that's it for NYC! But now let's cut back to what everyone's really concerned about: the quiet northern nation of Canada!!

Hey, Squirrelly Friends!

I just got done reading SG #11, and I feel like every new issue reminds me how much I love this friggin' series! This issue had everything that makes SQUIRREL GIRL so unique and enjoyable, from the rad humor to the organic way that you weave fun facts and actual computer science terms into the story in a plot-relevant way.

Which actually brings me to a point! (Yay for segues!) I should preface this by saying that I totally understand that you were going for a computer science angle on this, but would you believe me if I told you that there is an even more efficient way to count on one hand? It's true, dudes! In American Sign Language, you can actually count up to 999 before having to bring in a second hand! Pretty neat, right?

Anyway, I loved, loved, loved the issue, and I cannot wait to see Erica and Ryan at NYCC this year. Keep being your awesome selves!

Peace out, Squirrel Scouts,
Shani

RYAN: I know a bit of ASL and I considered mentioning that style of finger-counting, but it didn't fit the computer science theme of the issue! Alas. You already know this, Shani, but guess what, everyone else? ASL is an amazing language. When my wife and I are at a party and we want to see if the other one wants to go home, we sometimes catch the other's eye and discreetly sign "GO [to] HOUSE?" It's really easy: you can sign "GO" by pointing your index fingers on each hand at each other and rotating them around each other in a rolling motion, and "HOUSE" is just making your hands form the roof of a house and then bringing them down for the walls. Do it really quick and nobody will even know you're the kind of person who leaves a party to go home because you get sleepy sometimes! Technically we should be saying "GO HOME?" but the sign for HOME is less discreet.

ERICA: Hey guys, I know a lot about computer science and sign language as well! Just don't ask me any questions about them. What fun we're having talking about things we all know about. Anyway, did you know that New York Comic Con will be the FIRST TIME Ryan and I are doing a convention together??

Dear Erica and Ryan,

I have been reading and re-reading SQUIRREL GIRL many times over the last month or two, and am on a bit of a squirre(vangelica)l mission to share its wonders with my comics-loving friends.

I stayed at a lovely place called Looking Stead in the Lake District (UK) last weekend where

RED SQUIRRELS ARE AN ACTUAL FEATURE. Attached is a pic of my view at breakfast.

I have no idea if she's capable of kicking butts (crime being somewhat rare in them parts), but the other half of the theme song still seems to hold true.

P.S. The "squirrel" homonym puns don't work that well in the UK due to the difference in pronunciation. We're generally "squi-RUhl" more than "squrl." But that is like the only complaint I have about your comic so just keep being hilarious and I am sorry for bringing it up.

Unless Doreen comes to the UK, in which case IT IS ON (between squirrels, maybe).

Very much love,
Kevin

RYAN: I think Erica and I both SOMETIMES do a deliberate "Squir-RELL Guir-RELL" in the way we've heard people from the UK and Germany try to pronounce it so it rhymes. Two syllables for both "squirrel" and "girl"! It's actually very charming. Also, Kevin: Is crime rare in the parts where you saw the squirrels by chance, or could it be...the squirrels are the ones KEEPING the crime rate low?? Just something to think about in case you're planning to start stealing everyone's stuff in what I can tell you now is the delightful-looking Looking Stead in the Lake District.

ERICA: I love seeing other types of squirrels in the wild. I've always lived on the upper east coast so it's mostly eastern greys for me. Toronto is full of black squirrels. It's so cool. We'll be out in Leeds for the Thought Bubble comic convention later this year. I look forward to seeing what sorts of squirrels that trip will bring.

Dear Nutty Buddies,

After nearly two years, I was beginning to wonder when Erica was going to need a break, and I dreaded the idea of someone else coming along to try and fill her shoes. So let me just say how pleasantly surprised I was with guest artist Jacob Chabot's work in issue #11! And even without his sister from another mister, Ryan knocked another great issue out of the park too,

so kudos to both of you. From Doc Ock to K the College Administrator, this issue really f an homage to Squirrel Girl co-creator Steve in so many ways. I mean, if Doreen signal o'clock" in binary hand signs while def one of Doctor Strange's oldest villains, w turn is wrapped in the symbiotic flesh of Spider-Man's most powerful adversaries totally kick-butt tribute to one of Marvel's artist-creators, then I don't know what is thankfully, Erica wasn't completely absent this issue either, and I'm not just talking the final panel she drew. Her comment letters page about the best ever Nomad has secured her the highest place in my e for all time. Now, if you could just figure way to bring him back from the dead, N would be in his "Lazarus Lorenzo Lamas" which, of course, would be even better!

Darryl Eth
St. Catharine

P.S. I have to ask, do Doreen and/or Toe ever watch AMC's The Walking Dead so, how do they feel about Daryl Dixon's fa snack?

RYAN: Here is a thing: I wrote this because I like to have one-shot i between arcs where we can try someth little different, and it was already comp scripted when we realized Erica need time off to focus on the UNBEAT SQUIRREL GIRL BEATS UP THE MA UNIVERSE! book we're working on (whi already mentioned in the comic itself so i like I need to mention it again here BUT S And by complete luck, the next issue drawn already had a stand-alone story a different art style would fit perfectly W the narrative of the comic itself! Even th panel of Doreen sleeping was already scr all we changed was to have that one dra Erica. So it worked out really well AND knocked it out of the friggin' park.

As for The Walking Dead, I've only the Clementine games, so I'll have to d Erica's encyclopedia knowledge of tele on this one.

ERICA: Haha. It wasn't even a break. "OH NO I STILL HAVE HALF OF THIS 105 OGN TO DRAW AND THERE'S THE MO BOOK TOO? WHY DID I AGREE TO THI was sort of the opposite of a break. An luckily I was heading to Heroes Con (run very own Rico Renzi) right as we deci get a fill-in, so I spent the weekend sco I didn't even realize Jacob was there un

er-party and he was in my top two to do
ndipity!

restingly enough, even though I am
bingeing TV shows and horror movies
work (it just helps having something
oing on while I draw), I never got
to *The Walking Dead*. I haven't even
the game yet! Ask me any questions
Community or the *Hellraiser* series,
. Fun Fact: I don't put anything on
do layouts because there's too much
thinking there. Movies that I always
ell to: *Resident Evil*, *Naked Lunch*.

nd Erica,
is the first letter I have EVER written to
creators, and it starts out a little funny,
st me, it will make sense in a minute.
huge SG fan, even more so since you
rted working on it. I am also a STAR
fan. I have read everything, and I mean
ing STAR WARS. Even stuff like the
here the Emperor's illegitimate triclops
nds the glove of Darth Vader on an
ater planet and it gives him the ability
Force Lightning. Now Marvel has STAR
and the comics are great, and I love
But on the days where USG and a STAR
comic come out at the same time, I look
both. And without ANY hesitation at all,
up your comic and devour it while Poe
n sadly or Luke just sits there waiting
to get on with his story. I would once
ike to impress how much your comic
to me and the joy it brings. I have loved
WARS since I was 4, about 30 years
ut now it has to wait so I can see the
ne adventures the Unbeatable, CS-
Squirrel Girl and her amazing friends are
(Also, I can count to 31 on my fingers
ou guys rock!) Keep up the great work
ay the squirrels be with you!

Brad Woolwine
Austin, TX

N: Aw, Brad, this is great! Thank
ut now I really want to know about
clops son and what his deal is. Was
duoclops like most of us, who just
hieved? A quadroclops who lost an
low I'm gonna have to read the STAR
book, "The Tale of the Triclops and the
water Lightning Glove," which is what I
ely hope that book was called.

CA: Fun Fact: When I was a kid I
s insisted on playing as Han Solo but
had a lightsaber (large stick). I think
us had lightsabers actually, as long as
were enough sticks.

st wanted to say how much I love your
s! I can see myself in Doreen (and
el Girl) and I feel like if I were a super
'd be like her. I am currently working on
rel Girl costume for Halloween, despite
ow being "too old for dressing up"... I
you can never be too old for free candy,
Also, I NEED to see Squirrel Girl say,
! To the Squirrel Scooter!" :)

Nina G.

Milwaukee, WI
(P.S. Go Great Lakes Avengers!)

RYAN: Nina, you gotta send us pictures of your costume! You ARE never too old for candy (just ask my friend Joey, who – somehow?? – manages to survive on eating mostly candy) (KIDS: do not do this, there are Consequences) (ADULTS: don't do it either, I don't know how Joey hasn't turned into a giant Swedish Berry by now).

Speaking of the Great Lakes and their avenging thereof, I met Zac Gorman (he's writing the new GREAT LAKES AVENGERS book! It's gonna come out soon!) and we discussed SECRETS about Squirrel Girl, and now I'm super excited to see what the GLA get up to.

ERICA: WHAT? THERE ARE SECRETS? WHY DON'T I KNOW THESE SECRETS? Don't say that it's because they're secret, RYAN. Anyway, it is August as I type this and I'm already stressing out because my fiancé and I haven't planned out our matching Halloween costumes yet, so don't worry. Anyway, cosplay tips: Costume 1 is a halter body suit. Costume 2 is a tennis dress with capri leggings (because I got really excited that they make sports dresses but then I was like "these are so short you're literally jumping around and now everybody has seen your butt").

Ryan,
Some suggestions for Nancy Whitehead catchphrases:

Go for the eyes, Mew!
Stuck with ANSI? Here comes Nancy!
It's time to knit sweaters and pet Mew.
It's time to count stitches and engage in at times heated, albeit always rational, discourse!

Also, does Nancy have a middle name and does it start with "P" because then her catchphrase could be "You've got an NP problem to deal with now, buddy." /slickt/

That sound effect is an HP RPN calculator opening.

Erica, you are perfect in every conceivable way appropriate to the appreciation of your work by an old married man.

Please never stop,
Gary

RYAN: These are all solid catchphrases and I see nothing wrong with any of them! I do like the idea of Nancy taunting a bad guy by saying "Things are about to get hard for you, buddy. NP HARD." Fun Fact: I attended a lecture by Professor Cook – who introduced the P vs NP problem, which remains the greatest open question in computer science – at the University of Toronto! If you ask ME, P does NOT equal NP, but I, uh, don't know how to prove it. For those of us who don't have a ready knowledge of computer research to refer to, know this: Nancy's tagline is extremely excellent and if she ever fought someone who studied computational complexity theory, they would be very impressed by it.

ERICA: Gary is a smart guy. Real smart.

Dear Ryan and Erica,
I'm 9 years old and I LOVE, LOVE, LOVE the SQUIRREL GIRL comics! They're so funny! My dad and I go to our favorite comic book store and buy SQUIRREL GIRL comics along with my mom. I just recently had a SG comic book marathon with my guinea pig, Twix. She jumps around happily while I read out loud to her. Twix is going to be Tippy-Toe, my dad and mom are going to probably be squirrels, and I'll be Squirrel Girl for Halloween. Quick question: Does Twix look a bit like Tippy-Toe? Keep up the great work with these comics!!! (Attached is a picture of Twix.) #<3SG4EVER

Your Squirrel Girl Fans,
Isabel Mendoza and Twix
Las Vegas, Nevada

RYAN: TWIX LOOKS SUPER CUTE AND I CAN DEFINITELY SEE THE RESEMBLANCE. Also I love that you and Twix are going as Squirrel Girl and Tippy, respectively, and your parents are going as unnamed squirrels. That's what they get for not calling more exciting characters sooner!

ERICA: Dear Isabel, please send us pictures of Twix in a little bow. I suggest a tiny clip-on since I think most rodents will not deal well with a ribbon tied around them (Tippy-Toe is not most rodents). Also send us photos of ALL OF YOU IN COSTUME.

Next Issue:

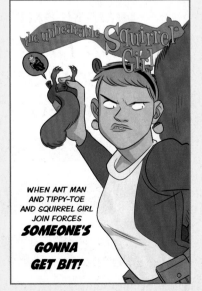

WHEN ANT MAN AND TIPPY-TOE AND SQUIRREL GIRL JOIN FORCES **SOMEONE'S GONNA GET BIT!**

the unbeatable Squirrel Girl

WHEN ANT-MAN
AND TIPPY-TOE
AND SQUIRREL GIRL
JOIN FORCES,

SOMEONE'S
GONNA
GET BIT!

Squirrel Girl *in a nutshell*

Squirrel Girl @unbeatablesg
guys i'm SO BORED, i'm up here in CANADA but there's NOTHING TO DO except read boring magazines

Squirrel Girl @unbeatablesg
and the magazines are SO BORING that i can no longer use punctuation or capital letters

Squirrel Girl @unbeatablesg
boredom has literally sucked the ability to use punctuation out of me

Squirrel Girl @unbeatablesg
science thought it couldn't be done

Squirrel Girl @unbeatablesg
but here we are

Squirrel Girl @unbeatablesg
me with internet: HI I'M COOL AND CAN DISCUSS SEVERAL INTERESTING SUBJECTS!!!
me without internet: i wonder what bark tastes like

Squirrel Girl @unbeatablesg
me with internet: I HAVE SEVERAL HOT TAKES ABOUT TODAY'S NEWS!!
me without internet: so it's decided: i can sneeze at least 3 different ways

Squirrel Girl @unbeatablesg
me with internet: CAN'T WAIT TO CHILL WITH MY PAL TONY STARK ON SOCIAL MEDIA
me without internet: me and that rock are bffs, don't @ me

Squirrel Girl @unbeatablesg
me with internet: WOW SO THAT'S WHAT MY ROBOT PAL BRAIN DRAIN IS DOING IN NYC!
me without internet: i have unsolicited opinions on gardening

Squirrel Girl @unbeatablesg
UPDATE: guys it's a few hours later and things are more interesting now!! There's a CRIME going on!

Squirrel Girl @unbeatablesg
Someone is stealing muffins from my mom!! It's the CASE of the MISSING MUFFINS and I am ON IT

Squirrel Girl @unbeatablesg
also yes I am aware of how pathetic this sounds but listen, I NEED THIS

Squirrel Girl @unbeatablesg
UPDATE 2: okay it turns out there's a whole city of tiny men living beneath our rental cottage who can split apart and back together

Squirrel Girl @unbeatablesg
and who are attacking us on sight for some reason that I don't know!! WHOA!!

Squirrel Girl @unbeatablesg
Anyway I queued these all to post when I'm back in a place that has FRIGGIN' DATA but I should really get back to it

Squirrel Girl @unbeatablesg
Can't fake being knocked out FOREVER, you know?

Squirrel Girl @unbeatablesg
Plus, these tiny Enigmos who are trying to tie me to the ground aren't gonna let me use my phone indefinitely, I'm pretty sure

search!

#canadafacts

#dontatme

#gardening

#thatsapaddlin

#enigmos

Somehow I always knew it would end like this.

Wait-- you hear that?

Chhtttt!*

Squirrels?!

CHOMP

Squirrel

*Roughly translated: "Attack, my Canadian cousins! Destroy the tiny men!"

Eugh.

Quickly before they merge togethe again!

Is this one of the guys you fight in New York City, Doreen?

No, *Mom*. And you can just call it New York!!

You never told me about him.

SCHLDORP

SMACK

This isn't "one of the guys I fight in NYC," Mom!!

It's fine if you don't tell me everything that's going on, Doreen, but I want to be there for y--

This is a new guy Mom

I promi this is a guy

This is the Canadian Forest: quiet, peaceful, serene...that is, until *Engimo the splitty-apart bad guy* wakes up! (He's a bad guy who splits apart into smaller bad guys wh also split apart, and now we're all up to speed.)

on, we're getting f here. Squirrels, on me!!

Wait, we're not staying to fight him?

Uh, you hit him and he splits into two smaller people. I know how this story ends...

...and I'm not sticking around until he's inside my *friggin' lungs*.

SWOOOSH

All right, I'll say it.

It's **weird** that your mom's rental cabin would be a super villain's lair.

Right?!

I don't understand why; there's nothing special about it. Of all places, why would he choose to go **here?**

...Because he didn't. *Frig.*

What?

Guys, what if those weren't the **only** versions of him running around? What if he didn't **choose** Northern Ontario, but we just ran into him because that's where **we** are? If he can split into tinier dudes...

...then there's no reason why they'd all have to stick together. He could be **everywhere.**

Exactly. And maybe he's here in the middle of nowhere because he's **already** expanded everywhere else.

We need to get into town.

e, what happens is he gets so small that air can carry him, and then you breathe in Engimo dust, and then you've got tiny Enigmos in your lungs that smush together to form a larger but still pretty tiny Enigmo inside your lungs. *Hard pass.*

The nearest town, not too much later...

Well, we're pooched.

I don't get it. How can there be more than one of him?

Anyone who can split apart and merge back together again has to be able to use their body like raw building materials. Split apart, visit a large enough buffet, merge back together, and you'll have enough biomass for a second dude.

Or two.

Or two thousar

DOODLEY DOO

Huh?!

?

Doreen!! Was that your incoming text noise?

Dude, check it out! We're close enough to civilization that our phones can get a signal!!

TAPPITY TAP

Q: How did Doreen avoid being seen? A: She scurried along the ground to the far side of the tree, and then leaped up to the branches, using the trunk as cover! We wo shown it but we've only got so many pages per issue, and we figured y'all already knew the specifics of tree-based stealth! You're *Squirrel Girl* readers. You got ✦

Uh, guys, I think you'll want to read this.

The news sites aren't doing much better.

SPIDER-MAN
hey anyone know what's going on?? same guy is everywhere at the same time? if it's cloning i'm gonna flip a table, omg

TONY STARK
Doreen, message me when you get this. We, uh, could use a hand.

THOR (LADY ONE <3)
Squirrel Girl, your digits come to me from Stark. I message now as we face an emergency of legendary proportions. Verily, hit me back.

HOWARD
soem guy calleld "enigom" juts toko over new yokr cityq but espelcicayly my ofifce, can u coem hepl me get ti back k thnkas!!!!1

HULK (AMADEUS CHO ONE):
SQUIRREL GIRL!! HULK whoa caps lock sorry! Squirrel Girl, Hulk here. We need you. We're being overwhelmed. Where are you?

GLOBAL MESSAGING SYSTEM:
ATTENTION CITIZENS: OUTGOING TEXT MESSAGING SERVICES ARE NOW PROVIDED BY AND TO ENIGMOS ONLY. WE THANK YOU FOR YOUR UNDERSTANDING IN THIS TIME OF TRANSITION. ENIGMO OUT.

NEW YORK BULLETIN
TOP HEADLINES:

Everyone In Power Is Enigmo Now...And That's Great!!

Vigilantism Is Now Illegal, All Remaining "Super Heroes" To Happily Stand Down Any Minute Now

Military Taken Over By Engimo! Public Relieved, Because It Was Actually Really Dangerous To Have All Those Weapons In The Hands Of Strangers

BREAKING: Enigmo Objectively a Better Leader than All Other Leaders Combined

Public Unanimous: New State-Controlled Media "Endlessly Perfect"!

PLUS: New "Life's a Laff with Enigmo" Special Comics Section

See, Mom? *See?*

This is what we get for staying in a place *without* internet!!

So are we--

Yes okay fine let's go fix it

kcikde me in teh btutt adn caleld me "quackres," whikc, like, *heollo* I've hearfd rthem all ebfoer! I've herads thme alol befoer, sqyulkrel guril!! waugh!!! anywya hti me bakc

Those "HNNNNK" and "HNHH" are snoring sound effects. I created them by listening to someone snore as they slept while taking detailed notes!!

Brain Drain is not a trained pilot, which is why he's ejecting instead of trying to land that jet. I thought about it and it's exactly what I'd do in that situation, which means it is extremely realistic, because I myself am also extremely realistic!!

Scott's just lucky that Maureen left all the cod, fiddle music, poutine, and dulse inside.

Brain Drain, you just--stole Ant-Man?

And a big chunk of my house, **and** the jet I was supposed to be securing!!

It was a **very** expensive jet.

I KNEW WE WOULD REQUIRE AN ALLY IN OUR FIGHT FOR JUSTICE, AND YOU WERE THE TOP CANDIDATE WHO WOULD ALSO FIT IN THE TELEPORTER WITH ME

didn't even **take** a teleporter! **You 'ole my jet** and then crashed it!!

I MUST CONFESS THAT I DID NOT CONSIDER THE POSSIBILITY THE PLANE WOULD NOT BE PROGRAMMED TO RETURN HOME. IF I MAY OFFER AN OPINION, THIS SEEMS TO BE AN OVERSIGHT ON THE PART OF--

Argh!!

Listen, **Robocop**, here's something **else** you didn't think of: I've got a **criminal record**, and now I'm in **friggin' Canada**. You know what a **pain** it's gonna be to get back **across** the border?? They've got **ant-sized cameras** built **just for me** now!

BORDERS ARE BUT IMAGINARY LINES, THE DREAMS OF WILD MEN WHO ONCE THOUGHT THEY COULD IMPOSE THEIR WILL ON AN INDIFFERENT WILDERNESS

They're also the dreams of border guards with guns who don't like it when people sneak across them!!

"Sure, Scott! You can go to bed early for once! You can definitely get a full night's sleep for once without waking up to your **country** being taken over by a splitty guy while your business is **sabotaged** by a **robot man** in an **unrelated disaster!**"

He took over Canada too, Scott.

Great, he got America's two-for-one too!!

o, it's been fun g kidnapped in **the middle** nowhere with a bunch of anadians--

Actually, I'm American, Doreen's got dual citizenship, and--

--but I'm out of here.

He knows the only way out of here is by canoe, right?

...I don't believe he does, no.

SLAM

There are some international borders that go right through the middle of cities, even buildings! Borders are **crazy**! Nobody tell Brain Drain though, it sounds like he's got enough opinions about them already.

come steal *your* bedroom and *your* plane and see how much *you* like it, leave *you* in a boring country full of nerds

nerds who can't even figure out how to build a *stupid* canoe that goes in a *stupid straight line*

SPLASH SPLASH SPLASH

Scott...
You wanna talk about it?

NO! I want to be *back in Miami* so I can help take *country back* from the weird *squishy man* that too over, and then *later* call up Mr. Jetman and *someh* convince him to keep giving me *business* even aft I got his plane *exploded* in *Canada!*

Here, let me help you. Come back to the dock.

I'm trying

Guys, you wanna grab the other canoe? I'm gonna help Scott.

We'll be right behind you. Nancy, which type of lifejacket do you prefer, near-shore or hybrid?

Uh...the type that's... the best?

Near-shore it is.

Scott, first, while Canadian law doesn't require a lifejacket or other personal floatation device be *worn* in a canoe or other human-powered pleasure craft, it does require that there be one available for everyone on board. And if you ask me, if it's on board, then you might as well wear it.

country chock full of nerds in lifejackets

And second, you want to hold the paddle with one hand at the top and the other near the middle, see? Let your *torso* rotate as you pull.

Go ahead-- I'll steer us, you just paddle.

half a mind just to shrink this whole country and call it a day, there's gotta be some downsides but i'm *really* not seeing 'em right now

That Canadian human-powered pleasure craft law is legit. Also, yes, Canadian lawyers call canoes "human-powered pleasure craft," which should tell you all you need to know about Canadian lawyers.

SLLP

So, uh...we've never formally met out of costume before. I'm Doreen Green.

Yeah, I know. Talks to ants.

Scott Lang.

SLLP

Well, animal-themed hero to animal-themed hero, we both know that's not fully accurate. I don't **talk** to ants. Nobody does.

Huh?

SLLP

I control 'em. Kinda like--telepathy, I guess, right? My helmet does the heavy lifting.

Which your robopal left behind in Miami, *incidentally.*

t, wait. You don't **ask** ants to do ything, you just **make** them do ? Like...like **mind control?**

Doreen, they're **ants.** And you're one to talk, you do the exact same with squirrels!!

No I don't! I talk to them. I **ask** them to help me out, and we **negotiate.** Mammal to mammal.

Hah! You're not serious.

...You're **not** serious, right?

Chukk chut chitt!

Exactly, Tippy! We talk about everything: crime-fighting, nut harvests, our big important feelings...

Oh my god, you're absolutely serious.

SLLP

y dog cries I ask him about his big important feelings, and he never replies, possibly because it's *really hard* to say "your big important feelings" and still sound sincere.

Whoa, this was *not* part of the Ant-Plan!!

Pretty awesome, Scott.

Right? Thank you. I was *going* to put the jet there for safe keeping this morning too, but *someone* kidnapped me before I could.

YES, HELLO, THE WORLD IS FULL OF CHAOS AND MADNESS AND ONE MAN CANNOT POSSIBLY SHOULDER ALL THAT BLAME

...we take the ...es to the far ...e, I carry us all ...e highway, and ...hightail it to America.

Yes. Perfect. Done.

But what'll we do once we arrive in the USA?

I dunno! We figure it out, form a team with whoever's there, take him down. There's gotta be a way.

Teams. **Yes.** Oh my gosh, it's an *ant* and *squirrel team-up*, together at last!!

SCHLOORP

I WOULD LIKE TO STRESS THAT THIS TEAM-UP ALSO FEATURES NIHILIST ROBOT MEN

And moms who are very proud of their daughter and love her very much, and who know she's gonna do her best just like she always does, and is certain she'll save everyone and do just great!

Mom!!

Oh my gosh--

SCHLOORP

--y'all are *far* too Canadian.

Sorry.

Anyway, OFF we go to America! While we *could* easily look behind ourselves right now, we all know there's nothing but an empty island there, so it's definitely not worth our time. Onward, friends!!

Chht! Chhit chukk?

Tippy's right. So how **do** we beat this guy anyway?

I have an idea.

Please, Nancy. I'm all ears.

So, Argentine ants. Invasive species. And in 2000, Japanese scientists discovered what they **thought** were a bunch of smaller colonies but were actually one **giant** ant colony, with 300 million workers and over a million queens.

Supercolonies! I read about these. A[nts] in one won't fight ea[ch] other, because they're [all] on the same team, eve[n if] they're in different ne[sts].

Exactly. But then we discovered another colony in the Mediterranean, this time spanning 3,700 **miles** of coast. And later scientists found the same thing in California. But here's the kicker: take ants from these different supercolonies, put them in a jar together, and guess what?

They **won't fight** each other either.

These ants, with an ocean between them, still behave like they're in a world-spanning **megacolony.** Sound familiar?

That's Enigmo's whole plan! If **he's** in charge everywhere, he won't fight **himself,** and hey presto: world peace.

Right. At the cost of everyone's freedom.

Wait, hold up. How do **you** guys know so much about ants?

General interest science reporting.

GENERAL INTEREST SCIENCE REPORTING FOR ME TOO

Dude, you never hear[d] of this? Scott, bu[ddy] you **gotta** read u[p on] your animal fami[ly]

But the megacolony's weakness is, even at **that** scale, there's always more ants **outside** the colony than inside it.

In other words, there's a lot of Enigmos around, but they're still fini[te]. The world's still full of sup[er] heroes. If we can make it to NYC, gather people there, if we can **organize...**

Look, I'm not saying ants are organizing themselves into a world-spanning superorganism. I'm just saying that when they **do**, y'all have no excuse for acting surpris[ed.]

Here Lies Ant-Van, 1975-2016, Beloved Friend of the Kra-Van, the Stilt-Van, and the Iron Van. She Will Be Missed.

Scott...

This is the worst "leaving me alone" I've ever seen, Doreen.

Look, I know it's bleak, okay? I know that we're in trouble, and that the Ant-Van was important to you.

...Her *secret* name was "Van-na White."

That's-- amazing, actually. But we're gonna pull this OFF, okay?

HOW, Doreen? We just got our butts kicked. It wasn't even a *contest*.

True, but look, Scott...I know we're not exactly the first group of people you'd call to stop Enigmo from taking over the Americas. So it's a good thing that's not what he's doing, huh?

I...don't follow.

We've been looking at this the wrong way! He's not trying to *take over* our countries, Scott. *He's trying to steal them.*

And what does someone with *your* skillset do when someone steals things from you?

...Steal them back, I guess?

Exactly. You just gotta see it like I do.

We're not a squirrel, a squirrel girl, a CS student, a brain in a jar on a robot body, a *mom*, and an ant guy.

We're the *infiltration specialist,* the *mastermind,* the *hacker,* the *muscle,* the *distraction,* and the legendary ex-con gone straight but sucked back in for *one last big score.*

HELLO

See?? All we're missing is the One Twitchy Person Who Says They're Fine To Pull Off A Heist, But You Just Know They're So Not Fine To Pull Off A Heist, and we'll be se

Next month: Catharsis! Escalating action! ...ding out why this one Enigmo has been stalking our gang! AND MORE??

Dear Squirrel Girl Crew,

Issue 11 was a triumph. I loved the numerical puzzles and the scene with Doreen caught in a final exam nightmare really hit home. I have a variation of her dream from time to time. There's a class I haven't attended and need to drop to avoid a failing grade. Trouble is, I can never find the building I need to go to in order to drop the class (and Nightmare is probably cursing himself for not adding that Kafkaesque touch for Squirrel Girl).

There was a little note on fan fiction. I just did a bit of that, if you are interested. In my previous letter, I said I'd like to see Squirrel Girl take on the White Rabbit. Via Amazon, I was able to buy the Rabbit's first appearance, Marvel Team Up 131. I did a customer review there, imagining the White Rabbit asking Marvel editors about the state of her career (she was not happy).

Sincerely,
Robert Fisher

RYAN: I saw a lot of people saying "HEY, I HAD THAT RECURRING DREAM TOO!" not realizing that it's pretty common. It's really common, turns out. Though not being able to find the building is a good twist. I'd tell dream-you to try doing it on your phone, I guess?

I am BIG INTO this fan fiction, and also, I am BIG INTO nobody correcting me on the error in #11! Thank you all for that. In case you missed it, there was a point where Doreen said that by using binary she can count to 1031 on both hands. If you tried it, you'll see this is incorrect: you actually only get to 1023! I'm not even gonna blame Doreen for this one: it was my fault! I just typed in the wrong number. But I wanted to mention it here, in case anyone got into "who can count the highest on their hands" competitions and then got stuck because of my mistake. Let this error happen… NO LONGER!!

ERICA: I've never dropped a class, so the version of the dream that I have is that I realize by mid term or finals that there's a class I never attended and I need to get there to try to make a last ditch effort to pass it but I don't know where it is or how to find the office that could help me (by this point the school has become a labyrinth).

Dear Unbeatable Squirrel-friends,

I AM SO HAPPY! Both the writing and art in this book just brightens my day every time it shows up in my pull-box! The writing is clever and these little human moments give me life. And Erica's designs and panel composition

match perfectly to really make SG Stand out from the other hero books out there!

I was so excited to meet Ryan at Zdarscon this year too, hopefully next time Erica is in Toronto I get to gush to her too!

Squirrel girl is a fun, totally rad character and thanks to you guys she keeps showing up in more places! Every time I show her to my friends they fall in love.

I hope she joins in on the fun for Monsters Unleashed! The whole concept seems to be made just for her!

Yes we Pecan,
Jakob Withakay

RYAN: Haha, so, I feel like "Chip Zdarsky Presents: Zdarscon" (pictured above in Jakob's photo) needs some explanation? But then I also feel like it works just as well if you have no idea what's going on! So, BASICALLY Chip (the same Chip from HOWARD THE DUCK! We did a crossover once! What a guy!) rented a hotel room and had his own mini convention in Toronto, and he invited me and a bunch of other friends to come greet fans and readers! He wore a bathrobe all day because it's his hotel room and who is gonna tell him what to do, and I wore my Star Trek pajamas because I will take any excuse to wear my Star Trek pajamas (Engineering division).

ERICA: SO. The last time I saw Ryan was the day after the Eisner award ceremony (WHERE WE WERE UP FOR TWO EISNERS *COUGH*). We were getting lunch and he tells me about these Star Trek pajamas and asks if he should buy them. I probably said something along the lines of "It's your money" and warned him that most pajamas aren't made for men who are 6'6". ANYWAY my point is that the moment they started posting photos from Zdarscon all I could think was "oh my god he did it. How do those fit on him?" That is Erica's story from home, 1 hour away (by plane) from Zdarscon. My fiance did ask if I wanted to go to Zdarscon but CHIP NEVER ASKED ME TO. I see how it is, Zdarsky. I see how it is.

Hi Ryan and Erica,

I just finished issue 11 – hilarious as usual! At first I was sorry to see Erica had a fill-in

artist, but was blown away by Jacob's
Any time you need a vacation Erica,
request Jacob to step in again. (Or
even a vacation? I have a sneaking sus
someone was working on what is sure
my new favorite original graphic novel.
wink!)

So, I had to write in and share a s
sighting with you all. I was hiking with a
on Assateague Island off of Virginia's E
Shore and was proselytizing about US
how he needed to read it. Lo and beho
crossed paths with the Delmarva Fox S
I wish I had gotten a pic, but alas I d
I don't think a photo would have do
animal justice though. In pictures it loc
a lighter-colored grey squirrel, but in p
it really does look like a fox except it
in the herky-jerky way that squirrels do
it was quite a bit bigger than a grey s
to boot!

Keep up the great work. Looking fo
to Unbeatable Squirrel Girl Beats U
Marvel Universe! Cheers,

Charles
Richmo

RYAN: Delmarva Fox Squirrel! Awe
You probably know this, but for eve
else: DID YOU KNOW that the Del
Fox Squirrel used to be on the endan
species list? But they're off it now
got them off the list by not destroying
habitat quite as much (always a good
you want to help), and by reintroducing
to new areas that we thought they'd d
in. They were added to the list in 196
they were taken off the list just a few m
ago, in November 2015! Another neat
about these squirrels is they don't hop
tree to tree, but rather climb down one
travel across the ground, and then cli
the next one. Safety first!

ERICA: Jacob is great. I'm so glad
was able to get him. I had A WEEKEND
a fill-in. Yeah, that month was basica
opposite of a vacation.

Squirrels I hope to see in real
Malabar Giant Squirrel, Japanese
Flying Squirrel, Jill the famous insta
squirrel, Theo the also famous insta
squirrel.

Dear Ryan & Erica,

I used to collect comics when I was yo
but I stopped about ten years ago. I've
back into them this year, and series like
are the reason why. As far as I'm conce
THE UNBEATABLE SQUIRREL GIRL i
best, most consistently high-quality
being published right now. I would go so
to say it's the best comic of the last deca

Given how good it is, I couldn't keep it [my]self. I've gotten my boyfriend into comics [a]nd Squirrel Girl is his absolute favorite.

Much love and admiration,
Eric (and Trevor)

[P].S. Is there any chance that Doreen's old [room]mates from the GLA will ever show up for [us]ue? Also, I hope we haven't seen the last [of] Sentinel Doreen dated!

[RY]AN: Eric, Trevor: thank you for these [very] kind words! I'm really glad you and [your] boyfriend like our talking squirrel [comi]cs. Hooray! As for the GLA — there's a [G]REAT LAKES AVENGERS comic coming [so]on! It's written by your friend and [mine] Zac Gorman, with art by Will Robson. [It loo]ks REALLY GREAT. As for the Sentinel, [we thin]k about him often and hope he's doing [well?]

[E]RICA: I think Doreen would say that they [are]n't dating, they just went on one date.

Dear Ryan and Erica,
[I] enjoyed the binary nightmare, but one [thing] strikes me, Doreen's diet doesn't seem [to ha]ve a hazelnut in every bite. What is this [odd] fascination? Are Doreen and Nancy [fe]d on grass? Or don't they know how to [eat] beans-on-toast or Marmite spaghetti like [re]al students? They will get rickets!

[Is]n't there a Spidey Student Survival book [with] Aunt May's wheatcake recipe? Or does [even] Morag need to spill the beans on how [to m]ake a poridggy? We need a sign on how [Squir]rel Girl gets her five day, if she is going to [be]in a beacon of clean living.

[N]ow that Doreen has taught the world to [coun]t, she needs to teach the world to cook, or [make] a Coke, which ever is easier.

Yours sincerely,

Simon Rogers,
United Kingdom

[P.]S Surely Mr and Mrs Nefaria were Count [and] Countess Nefaria, unless the current Count [boug]ht the title from one of those companies [that] sell plots of land on the Moon or surface [of th]e Sun?

[R]YAN: Simon, I would not put it past the [Coun]t to get suckered by one of those scams. [Fo]r Doreen's diet, I would actually really [like] to know Aunt May's wheatcake recipe. [Ther]e WAS a Marvel cookbook years ago [call]ed "Stan Lee Presents: The Mighty [Mar]vel Superheroes' Cookbook," because [of c]ourse it was) but it was published in [197]7 and includes recipes like "Spidey's [Cho]colate Web Pancakes" which tells you [to] "prepare pancakes according to the [instr]uctions on the package," put them [in a] stack, and then "form a web by criss-[cro]ssing lines with liquid chocolate syrup [acro]ss the top." There's also a recipe for [eas]y raisin bread" that is just "take pre-[slic]ed bread, push raisins into bread." In [con]clusion, I hope you enjoyed these two [deli]cious recipes.

[E]RICA: I'm not going to lie, I don't know

what y'all are talking about because I have been so busy that I never got around to reading issue 11! I still don't know how to use my fingers to count in binary! I'm just going to talk generally about food then. As a vegetarian, Doreen would have to be fairly conscious of her diet since her lifestyle more or less requires her to eat like a mini Dwayne "The Rock" Johnson but without depleting the oceans of cod. In this case falafel isn't a bad choice since beans and legumes are an excellent source of protein, something you're going to need if you're lifting cars on a regular basis. Nuts are also a great source of healthy fat and bursts of energy. Fun fact: Squirrels can't eat just nuts because they'll get too fat. They crave nuts because getting fat is good for the winter but they also need fungi, greens, fruits and insects. That's right! Squirrels are omnivores! They'll also eat snakes, other rodents and birds. So Doreen's vegetarianism is less about being like a squirrel and more about realizing that animals are sentient. I don't think that answered any questions you might have had but it's been so long I don't remember what they might have been.

Dear Ryan and Erica,
On Sept. 3, 2016, Squirrel Girl taught me how to count to 31 on one hand. Coincidentally, Sept. 3, 2016, was my 31st birthday. So, now, I am this many. Thanks Doreen.
Mike LaRowe (a.k.a. the Semi-Beatable Man Boy) in Grand Rapids (a.k.a. Beer City USA (for real))

RYAN: HAPPY BELATED BIRTHDAY, MIKE!! If we meet I'll give you a high five, or rather… a high thirty-one?

Dear Squirrely Duo,
I loved the Computer Science themed issue. Doreen knows the Powers of Two!

More CS fun:

```
if (you dare to pick a fight with Doctor Octopus) {
    you have sealed your fate
    for (i do not forgive) {
        i do not give up on revenge
    }
}
```

Since the 'for' loop has no exit condition, it

will run forever: "I do not give up…"
You left that as an easter egg for us, didn't you? Admit it!

I used to have the exam nightmare. But once, it was --math--. Looking at the first question, I could see what it was driving at. Even though I hadn't taken the course, I was able to derive the answer from what I already knew. Same with the second question. It was like being invited to explore a new mathematical domain, step by step. It felt wonderful! I turned in my paper knowing I had aced the test.

I haven't had that nightmare since.

Beat up the Marvel Universe? I'm only following two Marvel titles at the moment.
I'd like to see the Unbeatable Squirrel Girl kick back with the Unbelievable Gwenpool over pizza and sodas.

Very mostly yours,
John Prenis

RYAN: Man that sounds like THE MOST SATISFYING NIGHTMARE EVER IN TIME. I love it. I used to have Doreen's nightmare too, but I solved it like she did — talking to the Dean — and I haven't really had it since. But I barely EVER remember my dreams or nightmares, so it's actually kinda nice to have a nightmare and wake up, because then at least I get to remember my dreams! I have friends who have dreams that tell actual STORIES, and then when they wake up they can lift their dreams for stories they're working on, and I'm really jealous. They're literally getting work done in their sleep! MUST BE NICE.

ERICA: For a while I had episodic continuing dreams about having to stop an apocalyptic cult. Maybe we can use that? That sounds like our sort of thing. Marvel HAS A DUDE NAMED APOCALYPSE.

Next Issue:

14

Squirrel Girl *in a nutshell*

search!

#toronto

#cityhall

#heistmusic

#parentalleave

#physics

Squirrel Girl @unbeatablesg
Hey everyone guess who's back from her vacation in Northern Canada where she couldn't get a cell signal?

Squirrel Girl @unbeatablesg
And now she's in SOUTHERN Canada where she can easily get a cell signal, only this dude named Enigmo has taken over??

Squirrel Girl @unbeatablesg
And so now she's gotta deal with THAT baloney RIGHT AWAY even though she never got more than a few pages into Lake Enthusiast Magazine???

Squirrel Girl @unbeatablesg
Anyway yeah it's me. HELLO ENIGMO YOU SHUT DOWN SMS MESSAGING BUT WE CAN STILL HANG OUT HERE ON SOCIAL MEDIA

Squirrel Girl @unbeatablesg
anyway send me your freshest anti-Enigmo memes, as far as we know that could be his only weakness so it's good to be prepared I guess

Egg @imduderadtude
@unbeatablesg omg ive waited my whole life for this moment

Tony Stark @starkmantony ✓
@unbeatablesg Good to have you back. We, uh, haven't had much luck defeating this guy in NYC. He splits apart into other guys.

Squirrel Girl @unbeatablesg
@starkmantony Not a problem, Tony!! I once beat a guy made of a bunch of bees who could split apart into regular bees! NO BIG DEAL.

Tony Stark @starkmantony ✓
@unbeatablesg I can use this. What'd you do?

Squirrel Girl @unbeatablesg
@starkmantony Oh, bees can't fly when they're wet so I got him wet and then took bags of wet bees to the police. ANOTHER CRIME WELL FOUGHT

Tony Stark @starkmantony ✓
@unbeatablesg This...helps me precisely 0%.

Squirrel Girl @unbeatablesg
@starkmantony I'm on it, dude!! Me and Ant-Man came up with a plan to save everything! I can't tell you it publicly but let me just say

Squirrel Girl @unbeatablesg
@starkmantony WE ARE GONNA HEIST FREEDOM BACK

Squirrel Girl @unbeatablesg
@starkmantony ME and TIPPY and ANT-MAN and BRAIN DRAIN and MY MOM and MY GOOD FRIEND are gonna HEIST FREEDOM BACK

Squirrel Girl @unbeatablesg
@starkmantony AND IT'S DEFINITELY GONNA WORK

Squirrel Girl @unbeatablesg
@starkmantony AND WE'RE GONNA GO DO IT RIGHT NOW SO WHEN YOU NEXT HEAR FROM ME IT'LL BE ME SAYING "GLAD MY PLAN WENT PERFECTLY, LOL"

Squirrel Girl @unbeatablesg
@starkmantony I'm not sure if I'll say "lol" or not yet though

Tony Stark @starkmantony ✓
@unbeatablesg Yeah you always gotta play that by ear lol

Squirrel Girl @unbeatablesg
@starkmantony Tony

Squirrel Girl @unbeatablesg
@starkmantony It's weird when you do it

"MY MEMORY OF THESE EVENTS IS RECORDED WITH PERFECT, INESCAPABLE FIDELITY"

HEY GUYS.

Enigmo!!

YET AGAIN CHAOS SURROUNDS US, AND YET AGAIN I FIND IT TRAVELING WITH ITS TOO FAMILIAR COMPANION... INEVITABILITY

Dude, if we ever get back you gotta help me with my nihilism homework; this is *gold.*

Oh, it is *ON* now. Stay back, Squirrel Girl's mom!! *I'll* protect you!

NO, wait wait wait!

WEEOOP

I'm a *good guy!* I'm on your side!

Yeah right, chump!

No, I swear it! You can tell because I don't have the same scar on my nose all the other *bad* Enigmos have!

Hm.

Tiny Squirrel Girl on my shoulder, what do you think?

I think we should hear what he has to say, Scott.

I also think there are some *not unproblematic* concepts at play here equating innate goodness with the ideals of traditional beauty, but we can talk about that later.

OF *COURSE* there's an Empire State University course on nihilism. OF *COURSE* Nancy took that as her mandatory English elective.

"Here's the deal: years ago I was a star in the **Unlimited Class Wrestling Federation.** Remember them? Everyone in the league had powers."

"But *somehow,* people got tired of watching a rock man fight a man who can become tinier men. Sales dropped, and the league closed."

"And just li that, I wo homeles.

"I was stolen from, beaten up, attacked. People looked at me with everything from cold indifference to actual hatred.

"I saw humanity at its worst."

ANYTHING HELPS

"One day I was attacked by someone who wanted what little money I had. But when we all rejoined to fight our attacker...

Aah, my nose!

"...I didn't.

"I watched myself fight back. I watched myself get hurt. And then I watched myself leave.

"And that was it. I decided I'd had enough of people f a while. I lived off the grid. Eventually snuck into Cana

"And that's where I ran into you, on my little island."

CANADA: **50 MILES** (or 80.4672 of their precious "kilometers")

That island thing happened in *The Unbeatable Squirrel Girl #13,* which came out directly before this issue! Come on, man! *SERIAL STORYTELLING WORKS BEST IF YOU READ THE ISSUES IN ORDER, WE'RE TRYING HARD HERE BUT YOU GOTTA HELP US OUT AT LEAST A LITTLE!!*

...was easy enough follow you, since k like the people ower. You were ked by helicopter, by the way.

So you grew like a separate ant colony! A *good* ant colony!

All ant colonies are good ant colonies, Nancy. And Enigmo, sorry, I don't buy it. What puts you on *our* side when the others want to take over the world?

"Those of us born like this--there's no manual, t-Man. We all have to figure it out on our own.

"And there were times when I'd see the violence and bigotry and conflict in our world and figured 'You know what? I *could* do better.'

"I'd thought about taking over a lot. But then in my travels I found people who showed me kindness I never expected...

"...because I never saw it in myself."

"other me--he hasn't had those periences. He still thinks *he's* solution. He doesn't know what happen when you give people the chance to surprise you.

I want to help him, but first we need to *stop* him. And I know you don't trust me, Ant-Man, so I'm gonna tell you my greatest weakness, right now...

'Sup, bros?

...when split into r people, ny brain rs smaller, o. I mean, n I merge together emember ything they rienced, so e's definite vantages, ut yeah:

The smaller I get, the stupider I get. Get me tiny, and you'll be able to outsmart me no problem.

Actually, I can use that. You want a heist, Squirrel Girl?

Well, *here's* your *friggin'* heist.

Eeeeee

Can you tell an Ant-Man story and *not* have a heist in it? It is a question science is unable to answer, because the second someone tries, they're like, "Man, what if I just put a fun heist in here though??"

The Heist

"Step one: Enigmo splits off a tiny self, with a brain just big enough to remember two things...

"...that Squirrel Girl has come up with a way to beat him, and that she wants to meet him here in Toronto.

"Step two: Tiny Enigmo goes off and [...] the others, and every time another En[...] show up here to investigate, our Enig[...] merges with them and turns them go[...]

"Eventually we turn the majority, and then we win[...]

End of Heist

What?! What?! That's not a heist!!

♪♫ OOH, WE'RE PLANNIN' OUR HEIST, YEAH YEAH ♫♪

Heists are complicated, like clockwork, with perfectly timed distractions going off without a hitch! This is just two things happening! And they're not even happening in parallel!!

Plus you're only using the one guy! You're not even using the infiltrator, or the tech whiz or the muscle!

NOT TO MENTION THE WOMAN WHO'S REAL STRONG AND ALSO GOOD WITH SQUIRRELS?

WHICH IS ME, I MIGH[T] ADD??

See? Brain Drain played his heist-planning music. I can only assume you did the same. (For what it's worth, his song was "Planning Our Heist (Wow That's Nice)" by Sir Heist-A-Lot And His Three Pals Who Aren't That Into The Concepts Of Property Or Personal Ownership.)

I JUST ASSUMED YOU WERE TALKING ABOUT SOME OTHER WISE ELDER HEISTMASTER! I DUNNO, MAYBE MY MOM?

This is gonna be great, buddy. We are gonna empathize **SO hard** with conflicting points of view and reach mutually acceptable compromises. *YOU just wait.*

While studying with you, I could also split apart, read a bunch of books on debate and rhetoric, and then merge back together again.

Even better! Parallel learning!!

Okay, so all that's left is a place to lure them to.

We'll need a place that's got a large public square, in case several Enigmos arrive at once.

How about City Hall?

Welcome to TORONTO!

Our city hall has a large open public space out fron'

Not to mention lots of convenie' food trucks and souvenir stand'

Perfect. We'll also need a library, preferably nearby, so Squirrel Girl can help Enigmo complete his education as quickly as possible.

Billboard just to the right of the other one, dude.

Additionally, our city hall **ALSO** has a free library!

We're very proud of our socialized public services!!

'oud 'zed 'es!!

Plus, like all of Canada, we offer up to 50 weeks paid time off if you have a baby.

That's compared to the mere 12 weeks available in America, and that's **UNPAID** leave!

So what the heck, America??

These billboards are getting pretty sassy.

Sorry.

I don't think we expected Americans to see them.

So... heist is go?

Heist is go.

I'm not hold' my breath, but t' is at least a *ch'* this plan will wor' not fall apart a' immediatel'

America, I don't think having a baby is as cheap or as easy as your social safety net would seem to imply!!
SORRY, AMERICA, BUT BABIES EAT, LIKE, 100% OF THE TIME THEY AREN'T SLEEPING OR CRYING.

"AND THEN THE HEIST FELL APART IMMEDIATELY, REMINDING US ONCE AGAIN THAT THE ONLY TRUE CONSTANT IN THIS LIFE IS DISORDER AND CHAOS

"ANYWAY, HERE'S HOW IT HAPPENED

"PLANTING THE TINY ENIGMO WAS A SUCCESS, HOWEVER WE DID NOT KNOW THAT OUR ENIGMO HAD BEEN AWAY FROM HIS BROTHERS FOR TOO LONG. HE HAD BECOME TOO DIFFERENT, AND COULD NO LONGER MERGE WITH THEM"

Excuse me.

"SO WHEN THE ENIGMOS GOT WORD OF A TINY SELF THAT COULDN'T MERGE AND COULD ONLY SAY 'SQUIRREL GIRL KNOWS OF A WAY TO DEFEAT US AND WANTS TO MEET AT TORONTO CITY HALL' THEY NATURALLY ASSUMED SHE'D DISCOVERED A WAY TO BLOCK THEIR MERGING.

←OCCUPIED NYC
OCCUPIED TORONTO
OCCUPIED BRAMPTON

"WHICH WOULD BE CATASTROPHIC FOR THEM, SO INSTEAD OF SENDING A SMALL CONTINGENT LIKE WE'D HOPED, THEY ABANDONED MOST OTHER CITIES AND SHOWED UP HERE EN MASSE

VZZHHNNN

"I ESTIMATE AT LEAST 85% OF THE WORLDWIDE ENIGMO BIOMASS HAS GATHERED HERE IN TORONTO TO DEFEAT US"

ND ANYWAY, AFTER GIVING OUR ENIGMO A ENIR HAT SO WE COULD EASILY TELL HIM APART, QUICKLY DISCUSSING THE SITUATION WITH THE OTHER ENIGMOS, WE ENDED UP IN A FISTFIGHT

WHICH BRINGS US UP TO ABOUT NOW

Brain Drain, that was entirely unnecessary. My question was *rhetorical*, and we were all *there*.

TELLING A STORY IS ITS OWN JOY, AND WE SHOULD NOT BE SO QUICK TO DISMISS ITS PLEASURES IN A WORLD SUCH AS OURS

Making the good Enigmo look different was definitely not done just because it makes the good Enigmo easy to identify for you, the reader, when he shows up four pages from now. It *also* lets us draw and write about cool hats!!

Uh, clearly that guy does, Ant-Man. It's *right there*. Also, that's not the good Enigmo! *His* ball cap is red and has a maple leaf on it. We almost tricked you, huh?

ATCH

Mr.
.ang.

Mrs.
Green.

This doesn't seem to be working, Mr. Lang.

I noticed that, yeah.

Normally in situations like this, I'd just get giant and start stomping. But these guys just split apart when stepped on, so *that's* pointless.

I was wondering, Scott, how does that work?

, see, I get giant, and *then* I step on hings that are a problem until, *uh*, until they're not a problem anymore.

, I mean, what stops ou from collapsing der your own weight? sunflowers fall over en they get big unless I've staked them.

Oh! Pym Particles. They adjust the Planck constant, the Higgs Field, *and* the space between atoms while also shunting matter between here and a place called "the Kosmos Dimension." It's all very scientific.

Uh, allegedly.

Wait, *that's it!* Scott, that's how we win this!!

...huh?

Maureen! You are the *best mom* I've er met outside my own family, nd Scott, you're, *uh*, you're ctually pretty decent too for a guy who yelled at me about a van!

Thank you, Nancy.

Yes, well, I'm actually still really mad about my van.

I've got a note here from Deadpool from the last issue. It reads as follows: "CALLED IT."

Doreen, this is Nancy on top of City Hall! Leap out of earshot for a second so you can talk without Enigmo hearing what you're saying!

On it!!

Brain, I gotta take a call. I'll be right back, I promise.

THOUGH THIS FIGHT IS CLEARLY FUTILE, I FIND IN ITS FUTILITY A WELCOMING EMBRACE, COMFORTING IN THE SAME MANNER AS A FAVORITE SWEATER, OR A CALMING GAZE INTO THE ABYSS, WHICH, I REMIND YOU, GAZES ALSO

Yep!!

hup!

AND NOW I TURN MY ATTENTION BACK TO YOU, ENIGMOS, AS WE RESUME OUR FRUITLESS EXERTIONS, THROWING OUR BODIES AGAINST EACH OTHER IN THE MAD HOPE IT SOMEHOW CALMS US

Everyone! If we pile on top of this guy, maybe it'll shut him up for a bit!!

So you remember the tree lobster you fought, right? He was *fine*, right?*

Tree... lobster??

Yeah, man! Poor li'l guy got exposed to cosmic rays a became gian But other th that, he was just a lovabl critter.*

*This was covered in *Squirrel Girl Vol. 2 #8!*

Exactly. He became giant with *no problem*, thanks to cosmic rays. And when Ant-Man's giant, it's *Pym Particles* that do the heavy lifting to stop him from collapsing under his own weight.**

**This was covered on page ago. Ant-Man sa it! Come o

Oh, my gosh, I see where you're going with this.

GALILEO'S SQUARE-CUBE LAW FROM PHYSICS CLASS!!

Nancy and Squirrel Girl both know what that square-cube law is, but do you? Naw, me neither. But instead of throwing this comic away in a fit of *incandescent rage,* let's all keep in mind that there's a small chance this might be explained on the very next page!

Not necessarily giant mechas, but giant mechas if necessary.

And so...

I admit, I misjudged squishy guy. I did not think the giant bad guy would split apart into a bunch of smaller good guys with broken ankles.

...they *are* good guys now, right?

Yeah, Good Enigmo debated them, but nobody got to see anything because it was "an invisible rhetorical battle" on "the mental plane."

But whatever! They had a big debate at the speed of thought and concluded, "Oh hey, we just got beat by a robot man, an ant man, a squirrel lady, an actual squirrel, and two other ladies who are also awesome but just in ways that can't be summarized by a single adjective."

"*Wow, maybe there's something to this diversity thing after all??*"

But--it's over, just like that?

We thought we could save the world by replacing it with ourselves. It's not the way.

Instead we're gonna work *within* it to make it the best place it can be for all of us!

That's the beauty of a merged mind: convince one, convince them all. The others are gonna go out and turn the leftover Enigmos that didn't make it to Toronto, but yeah, this is over.

So...we can *finally* go? We can *leave* Canada??

Yes, Scott. Eventually, once we help all the Enigmos get their legs set...we can leave Canada.

Oh thank God.

All right, Enigmos! Whoever wants to get shrunk down and carried in my pocket back to America, *climb aboard the Scott train!*

Because this train is *leaving the station* and it is *never* coming back!!

You know, Doreen, he's single, *and* he owns his own business...

MOM

NO

OH MY GOD

The En[d]

Did you know: Toronto's actual slogan is "Diversity Our Strength"? I only realized that halfway through writing this story! And now you've got one more "Fun Canada Fa[ct]" in your brain, *PLUS* a bonus "Semi-boring Ryan Fact" too!

SQUIRREL GIRL, NANCY, TIPPY, AND MAUREEN FINISHED THEIR VACATION IN NOVA SCOTIA, FAMOUS FOR ITS FIDDLE MUSIC, STRIKING NATURAL BEAUTY, ACADIAN CULTURE...AND REMARKABLY FEW SUPER VILLAINS.

CANADA

TO ANT-MAN

THE CANADIAN GOVERNMENT GAVE ANT-MAN A BONUS FOR NOT SMASHING UP THE ENTIRE CITY HALL WHILE SAVING IT, WHICH HAPPENED, TO BE FOR THE PRECISE AMOUNT ANT-MAN OWED FOR HIS LOST PLANE, SO THAT WAS NICE.

...OTT'S ROLE IN SAVING THE WORLD GOT HIS BUSINESS A LOT OF ATTENTION...

...ENOUGH TO EASILY AFFORD A REPLACEMENT ANT-VAN.

BRAIN DRAIN CONTINUED TO FIGHT CRIME AND HIS OWN ENNUI IN NYC...

...BUT NOW IN A NEW COSTUME MADE FOR HIM BY MAUREEN.

...NIGMO DENOUNCED TRYING TO REPLACE ...MANITY WITH HIMSELF, AND INSTEAD, 14% ...HIS TOTAL BIOMASS PURSUED A MASTERS DEGREE IN THEORETICAL PHYSICS.

SCIENCE EVENTUALLY RECOVERED FROM BEING ABUSED BY BOTH PYM PARTICLES AND COSMIC RAYS, AND CONTINUES TO BE THE BEST WAY TO EXPLORE THE WORKINGS OF OUR UNIVERSE.

THE (REAL, FINAL) END.

You folks get many letters from young girls in whose lives you have been important, which is great. I am not a small girl. I am a guy who is approaching 50. Squirrel Girl is very important to my life.

For the last few years, I have been dealing with chronic pain, unemployment, and (unsurprisingly) depression. The Unbeatable Squirrel Girl has made me *literally* laugh out loud a bare minimum of once every single issue, often more. (Most recently with "So I cannot give it my full recommendation.") Laughs can be hard to come by. You deliver.

No pressure,
Alexx

RYAN: Alexx, thank you so much. That's what we're here for! I've got a friend with chronic pain and it is such a daily struggle, so to have unemployment and depression on top of that -- it's rough, dude. I know what we do is small in the grand scheme of things, but I'm really happy that we can help you out, even a little!

ERICA: I think one of the things that has surprised me the most is the range of people who have told me they enjoy the book. I'm really glad that we could make something that has positively affected your life.

Ryan and Erica:

Your mention of Koi Boi heading off to visit the ruins of the underwater kingdom of New Atlantis brought a couple of questions to mind:
1) Will you be presenting that as a Squirrel Girl special episode? There are usually technology raiders searching out hidden Atlantean technology in their ruins (not to mention trying to find Atlantean skeletons to sell on the alternative medicine black market). Surely Koi Boi is likely to run into one of them. If not, a guided Visitors' Board tour of the ruins might be quite beautiful. Unfortunately, I can't remember which destruction of Atlantis this ruin is from. Was it bombed, nuked, or biologically destroyed? Hmm, why was Koi Boi going there again?
2) Koi are fresh water fish. New Atlantis is in salt water. I seem to remember Koi Boi swimming in the harbor area so I assume that he can breathe heavily polluted salt water but can he also breathe fresh water? Does his amphibious nature allow him to breathe both? Does he have to use special

breathing equipment in one water or the other? Did Tony Stark make the salt filter / infuser unit for him? Man, this would make a really interesting Biology 201 class at his college!

Thanks for an entertaining comic,
Geoffrey Tolle
Lord of Squirrels (as soon as I start my 40 generation domestication project).

RYAN: 1) I don't think we'll show it! Normally I'd say "use your imagination," but you have clearly already done this, so I guess all I can say is "thanks for using your imagination!" If you could fill out that plot to 20 pages and send over a script, I'd be happy to take the credit for it!!
2) I think Erica and I discussed this and we agreed Koi Boi could breathe both salt and fresh water, but I admit we did not work out the specifics! Although MAYBE the fact that the original Atlantis is in fresh water is the reason everyone's had such a hard time finding it! MAYBE??

ERICA: I'm pretty sure he's good in all types of water. He can talk to all the fish and really just had to pick one to go with for the name. "Fish Boy" just doesn't cut it, you know?
Guys, Atlantis was built on the ruins of the original Atlantis 8,000 years ago. Anything that was there from the Great Cataclysm is surely in an underwater museum or merged into the new construction (like Rome) by now.

Ryan and Erica,

Wow guys, this comic is just swell. Squirrel Girl is truly unbeatable, and Nancy is such a rad character, and Koi Boy and Chipmunk Hunk are undeniably the most perfectly named super heroes ever. And geez, Brain Drain is just trying so hard to be a good superhero and I just...I just want him to be happy. I love you, Brain Drain, and I will always be proud of you. No matter what.

Squirrelfully Yours,

Elisha Smith
Knoxville, TN

RYAN: Aw, thank you! I -- I really love Brain Drain too. I am surprised at how cute he is, and I love how Erica has turned a literal brain with a pair of eyes attached into somehow the most facially expressive character. SHE IS MAGIC.

ERICA: I love our crazy nihilist [...] trapped in a robot body trying to be a s[...] hero.

Dear Letters From Nuts,

I wanted to draw attention to an app[...] discrepancy on the cover of issue #11. T[...] the binary numbering is displayed i[...] digits, 001011, whereas five digits, 0[...] would seem more applicable, since Do[...] teaches Count Nefaria (and us readers) [...] to count in binary on a single hand, [...] five fingers equal five digits. Sidenote[...] English word "digit" comes from the [...] word for "finger" -- how appropriate!

At first, I thought the cover numb[...] might have something to do with squ[...] having six fingers, but a hasty Google i[...] search revealed that four front fingers [...] five hind fingers are the usual sc[...] characteristics. I flipped through the [...] again and found no evidence of polyda[...]

Then it dawned on me: the six [...] binary numbering must have come [...] Doctor Octopus, who is right there o[...] cover. Raising one arm and the two opp[...] tentacles while keeping his other [...] not-being-used-for-standing append[...] lowered is naturally how Doc Ock v[...] flash his digits!

Does this explanation entitle me to a[...] Prize? I do hope so! I've long aspired t[...] rank of Titanic True Believer (T.T.B.), [...] would in turn bump me up to Perma[...] Marvelite Maximus (P.M.M.).

Morris Tichenor, R.F.O., Q.N.S., [...]
Toronto[...]

P.S. More etymology fun: the Latin [...] "digitus" probably derives from "[...] (meaning "to speak" + the suffix "-it[...] I like to image Romans gesticulated v[...] whenever they spoke.

P.P.S. I want to second Erica's asse[...] that Nomad's Lorenzo Lamas phase is [...] BEST Nomad." Thanks for giving a s[...] out to one of my favorite '90s titles.

RYAN: Man I love a letter that start[...] with "HERE IS A PROBLEM" and ends [...] "NEVERMIND, I HAVE COME UP WIT[...] SOLUTION TO THE PROBLEM THAT [...]

RES YOU PRETEND THAT YOU WERE
TER THAN YOU ACTUALLY ARE,"
is something I am more than willing
and may actually already be doing.
my understanding that No-Prizes are
IS VERY THING, which makes me
ely excited about No-Prizes. My
standing that they're just pictures
pty envelopes makes me LESS
d, but, well, here we are. (Also the
d zeroes worked nicely from a design
ctive, so really, TWO good reasons
that way.) ENJOY THE PRIZE:

CA: I... still haven't read #11, but
important is that the issue you're
tly reading got to the printers by the
ne.

really hoping that now that Steve
the run in the Marvel Cinematic U,
going to get at least a moment of him
s hair grown out riding a motorcycle
d. I know that he wasn't Nomad
that time, but we have to work with
we're given. Also, we know he can
motorcycle.

Squirrel Girl Crew:

njoyed Squirrel Girl's run-in with the
Man. It looks like next month, we
xpect Dr. Octopus and Venom. While
el Girl certainly has taken on some of
's big name villains, I recently became
ted in one of the lesser lights. Might I
st that Squirrel Girl versus the legend-
-own-mind White Rabbit would have
great possibilities?

Sincerely
Robert Fisher

AN: The time delay on these letters
s you have already (hopefully!) read
mic and seen what happens! Doc Ock
enom are two of my favorite bad guys,
as a treat to put them both in the same
(KINDA, AGAIN, I CAN ONLY ASSUME
READ IT BUT DON'T WANT TO SPOIL
HING). In any case, to answer your
on, I just looked up the White Rabbit
he has a giant robot rabbit that fires
es, so I'm already totally down with
hole thing.

CA: If you've read this issue, it
bly means you just finished a three-
arc starring a character who has only
in TWO OTHER ISSUES IN ALL OF
EL'S 70+ YEAR HISTORY. We're into
ep cuts too, is all I'm sayin'. I feel
ne of the hardest parts of doing this
ing who the villain will be each time.
literally going through that right now
ng for issue #17. I feel like this is
e thing we have trouble agreeing on
imes.

Another cracker from Ryan and Erica -
kicking off with Spider-Man getting in on the
Twitter conversation - and who is he kidding
when he says that his webshooters make
that "thwip" sound? We know that just like
Wolverine, he makes that noise himself.

Count Nefaria was wonderful and the
footnotes were right, we were all doing the
counting on our fingers too. Very elegant
solution to the nightmare about exams,
which we've all had.

There are lots of good comics about at
the moment, but Squirrel Girl, each and
every issue is just a JOY. Easily the nicest
lead character around - and isn't it lovely to
show that you don't have to be dark or angsty
or driven to be a compelling lead - you can
actually be kind and perky too.

(Jacob - the facial expression on Count
Nefaria's face in the "no way, you've got to
teach me" panel was just perfect)

Many thanks

Andrew Pack
Brighton, England

RYAN: Yeah, Jacob did a terrific job on
that issue, and I loved that we got to show
that Doreen's dreams are a little brighter
than the real world. That seems to fit, you
know? Thank you for all these kind words,
and I can only hope that future authors
continue to characterize Count Nefaria
as "a Dracula who likes numbers." IT
WORKS, YO.

ERICA: I was so glad we got Jacob. I
went to Wil with two names for who I'd like
to use and Jacob wasn't even sure he could
do it at the time, but we diiiiid iiiiit.

Dear Ryan, Erica, & Rico,

I first started reading Unbeatable Squirrel
Girl after seeing a copy of the 1st volume
at my library and thinking, "well, this looks
ridiculous but potentially fun." Turns out it
wasn't ridiculous (ok, maybe a little bit, but
absolutely in a good way), and was more than
just fun. I've been hooked on the adventures
of Doreen, Tippy-Toe, & co. ever since. So
much so that I cosplayed as Squirrel Girl for
NYCC this year, and actually got to meet all of
you (which was awesome)!

One of my favorite things about Squirrel
Girl is that she doesn't just use the powers
of squirrel, but those of girl as well. I love
a good superhero fight scene, and Doreen
can definitely kick butt (it's right there in her
catchphrase) but my favorite moments are
the ones where she uses reason, friendship,
and sometimes even computer science to
save the day. It's so refreshing to see a clever,
optimistic, and ultimately inspiring superhero
like Squirrel Girl who knows that it's often
better to talk things out and solve problems
with brains rather than fists.

Keep on eating nuts & kicking butts (and
writing amazing new stories for Squirrel Girl)!

Rachel

P.S. I wish I could've gotten a photo with
Rico too, but my friend had wandered off

with the camera. Thank you so much for the
button though, Rico! No one has asked me
about my squirrel powers yet, but I remain
hopeful.

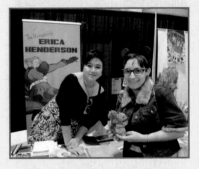

RYAN: Rachel, it was SO GREAT to meet
you at NYCC! At that show I was given my
very own stuffed Tippy-Toe by a fan, so
now I can pass as -- well, not Squirrel Girl,
but Squirrel Earl at least. Your costume
is amazing, and this letter is the best. I
like the photo with Erica the best because
it shows off your tail -- IT WAS A REALLY
WELL-MADE TAIL, EVERYONE! Fun fact:
NYCC was the first time Rico and I met in
real life, and then later on we all went out
to dinner and ate delicious guacamole. WE
LIVED OUR BEST LIVES THAT DAY.

Next Issue:

15

Squirrel Girl *in a nutshell*

search! 🔍

#zcrg5ju7,i;

#lknmjguifte4w3q

#zcdvtnmukil;;;;;;;;;;

#8dfuetryt3#4

#cyuu6ui7jjmmm

Nancy Whitehead @sewwiththeflo
zcadfewg5ttyniu,o;

Nancy Whitehead @sewwiththeflo
Hey everyone, sorry, my cat got on my keyboard and somehow posted that. Pretty cute though, right? Anyway, test post please ignore.

Nancy Whitehead @sewwiththeflo
';,l;joih87t67r5d4dsaqzdx

Nancy Whitehead @sewwiththeflo
Once more, sorry, Mew walked on my laptop again. Less cute the second time. I'll keep it closed from now on.

Nancy Whitehead @sewwiththeflo
hrzayus5f3iu6t54h76p8k70[k98;'--]\

Nancy Whitehead @sewwiththeflo
Okay okay she got on my phone this time but I PROMISE Mew will stop posting on my account.

Nancy Whitehead @sewwiththeflo
Thank you all for following me on social media today and I hoped you enjoyed this unscheduled #content.

Nancy Whitehead @sewwiththeflo
fmgnsjkbehrftyqu27334dfd5yn7c5jmikn,ob,lm;n9',

Nancy Whitehead @sewwiththeflo
Mew, how is this happening

Nancy Whitehead @sewwiththeflo
How is this happening, Mew

Nancy Whitehead @sewwiththeflo
XSCDV32CDN43KJ54HK6LUUMIK9OP97LKI

Nancy Whitehead @sewwiththeflo
Sorry, I'm sorry, I don't know how this keeps being a thing. I put my laptop under the bed WHILE LOGGED OUT, and yet here we are??

Nancy Whitehead @sewwiththeflo
VDSABCwvce32j43t56hy86jk98..l;jk

Nancy Whitehead @sewwiththeflo
Look all I can say is: if you followed me on this site then you knew the risks.

Squirrel Girl @unbeatablesg
@sewwiththeflo Maybe you should ask Mew to put her social media posts on... PAWS

Nancy Whitehead @sewwiththeflo
@unbeatablesg xacf435hy6gngj7ti7tj

Nancy Whitehead @sewwiththeflo
@unbeatablesg OKAY SHE'S REPLYING TO YOU NOW, HOLY COW, THIS IS CRAZY, WHAT IS GOING ON

Squirrel Girl @unbeatablesg
@sewwiththeflo I agree it's...CLAWS for concern

Nancy Whitehead @sewwiththeflo
@unbeatablesg I THINK I FIGURED IT OUT, YOU HAVE TO HIT CTRL+ENTER TO POST AND HER NATURAL GAIT REACHES THOSE TWO KEYS

Squirrel Girl @unbeatablesg
@sewwiththeflo but how is she getting the laptop open though??

Nancy Whitehead @sewwiththeflo
@unbeatablesg Listen, Mew is the best cat and therefore I'm sure she has her ways, but I'm CERTAIN now I've figured it out.

Nancy Whitehead @sewwiththeflo
@unbeatablesg It won't happen again. EVER.

Nancy Whitehead @sewwiththeflo
zwdreh4u7oi98p-['9=-=;p0lomnybtcdexweaq

Nancy Whitehead @sewwiththeflo
MEW

Nancy Whitehead @sewwiththeflo
WHY

Nancy Whitehead @sewwiththeflo
WHY, MEW

The End.

Ryan, Erica and Rico,

Thank you for all of the hard work, talent and dedication you all put into this wonderful, wonderful book each month. It had been nearly fifteen years since I've picked up a print comic every issue without fail, but your book has brought me back into the fold.

After your first issue #1 I made THE UNBEATABLE SQUIRREL GIRL a habit very specifically so that I'd have a box of comics to share with my daughter as soon as she's able to flip through them. I've become assured that I made the right choice for two reasons. First of all, you folks continue to produce an amazing, smart, insightful and funny all-ages comic and you show no signs of slowing down. Second, she's only eighteen months old and is absolutely obsessed with acorns. Every time she goes outside we wind up finding a few acorns around the living room later. Doreen must have some tough-soled shoes, because I swear those acorn caps are worse than Lego bricks to step on.

Nuts to you all,
Daniel and Carolyn Tauber

RYAN: Aw, that's great! I've got a nephew too who just turned three and while he's not quiiiite at the point yet where he's reading comics, I'm really excited for him to start. I am SO READY to be the cool uncle. I've got comics in my house, I've got lots of neat toys and a giant lime green stuffed T-Rex from *Dinosaur Comics* **– I AM READY. Perhaps he'll be reading this letter column in a few years and be like, "A time when I was so young that I didn't read comics? IMPOSSIBLE." ALSO: I didn't know stepping on acorn caps was worse than stepping on Lego, but I am happy to take your word for it and would absolutely not like to find out with personal experience.**

ERICA: Pro tip: glue down the caps. I learned this from cosplayers and jewelry makers. But yay! I'm glad we could get you back into comics and have provided you with something you can share with your daughter in the future.

Thank you for coming to Lethbridge Word on the Street and the signing at

Kapow. My husband and I have been fans of your work for years and are so excited that you are involved in an incredible Marvel comic. I wish we had some better pictures of our Unbeatable Squirrel Boy but he was also very excited.

Miranda
Alberta, Canada

RYAN: Miranda, THIS WAS THE BEST. Your Squirrel Boy was truly unbeatable, and it was hilarious how the second he was dressed up he ran off (because he was shy? Because ADVENTURE BECKONED??). Everyone else: If you've never been to Lethbridge, Alberta, Canada, I recommend it! I went for a walk while I was there and came across HENDERSON LAKE, which I can only assume was named after Erica Henderson, so I instantly felt welcome and at home.

ERICA: That lake thing is probably correct.

Ryan and Erica,

Wow guys, this comic is just swell. Squirrel Girl is truly unbeatable, and Nancy is such a rad character, and Koi Boy and Chipmunk Hunk are undeniably the most perfectly named super heroes ever. And geez, Brain Drain is just trying so hard to be a good super hero and I just...I just want him

to be happy. I love you, Brain D
and I will always be proud of yo
matter what.

Squirrelfully Y
Elisha S
Knoxvill

**RYAN: Thank you, Elisha! ¡
Drain believes in himself and ʈ
his best, and that is all anyon«
ask!**

**ERICA: My only regret is tha
didn't get to do more scenes of !
Drain in his human costume.**

Ryan and Erica,

Thank you so much for makir
realize how awesome Squirrel G
Your comic makes me crack up
time I read it, especially the "
Nutshell" segment from Issue 1
quite possibly one of the best cc
I've read! Squirrel Girl is, than
this comic, my favorite Marvel h
mean, come on! She's beat up Th
Galactus, and even the entire M
universe! Anyways, once again, 1
you guys!

**RYAN: Thanks, Ethan! I r
enjoy writing the "In A Nuts!
recap pages, and I also like
all the accounts there are re
would argue it makes total s
that Tony Stark, international
and billionaire, would hang
online with Doreen Green.
if you haven't picked up our
UNBEATABLE SQUIRREL GIRL B
UP THE MARVEL UNIVERSE! ori
graphic novel (it's an all-new st«
then what are you waiting f«
don't want to spoil anything, bı
say this: the Marvel Universe
absolutely get beat up.**

**ERICA: Aw! Thanks! We like I
lot too.**

"In this world, even a brain in
in a robot body can only do so m
You took the words right out c
mouth. Nicely observed! Brain [
Brain Drain, Brain Drain. He's
it. Were he a man, he'd be my !
He brings the pain! His reign

disdained! He brings a presence [on] his plane that others only feign! If [you] mess with him you best be prayin'! [Yo]u, like that.

[Ry]an North and Erica Henderson, you [two] are still rocking it like a magikist. [...] Renzi and Travis Lanham and Wil [...]s are doing this as well. I'd like to [...]rate - this time into lettercol canon [tha]t Ryan "Ry No" North should have [thou]ght a duo composed of the Rhino [and] a new villaness named the Air-Hen. [For] no reason I can explain, the latter's [villai]n name should be Peppy Bosworth.

Keep it up!
John Velousis

[R]YAN: John, this Brain Drain [the]me song is a thing of beauty. And [PER]SONALLY, I think the Rhino (who [is alr]eady a Marvel villain, so: CHECK) [and] the Air-Hen should team up and go [on a]dventures. Erica, do you want to [go o]n an adventure? We are currently [in Le]eds in the United Kingdom for the [Thou]ght Bubble convention, so I guess [we're] already on one??

[E]RICA: I love how much people love [Brai]n Drain. It hadn't even been that [long] since we introduced him but I [was] already dying to bring him back. [Rya]n and I were having breakfast [adve]ntures in Leeds. Who can eat the [mos]t breakfast?? (Ryan. Ryan can.)

[He]y, True Believers,

[I t]hought you might appreciate the [Squ]irrel Girl costume my wife helped [mak]e for my 10-year-old daughter [Fion]a. Happy Halloween!

[(A]nd yes, those are totally comics in [the b]ackground.)

James VanOsdol
Chicago, IL

costume is unbeatable and I certainly hope at Halloween when people opened their doors and saw her they just emptied their entire bowls of candy into her pillowcase. I WILL ACCEPT NOTHING LESS.

ERICA: I hope those bats are year-round décor. Fun times goth house. ANYWAY – Fiona looks great! This makes me happy because I don't think I've seen trick-or-treaters since I left for college. Halloween is not just for rowdy adults, people!

Okay, that's all the room we have this month. DO NOT MISS THE NEXT ISSUE! Why? Because it's a special celebration of the 25th anniversary of Squirrel Girl's first appearance! With a short story by none other than SG's co-creator Will Murray! And you'll maybe (MAYBE!) even learn Squirrel Girl's origin!!!!!!!!!!!!!!!!!!!!!!!!! (And yes, that was twenty-five exclamation points.)

Next Issue:

the unbeatable Squirrel Girl

16

Squirrel Girl in a nutshell

search! 🔍

#meetcute

#followtheleaper

#monkeyjoe

#properconcussiontreatment

#fishyhulk

#avengersassemble

Squirrel Girl @unbeatablesg
IT'S MY BIRTHDAY!! I'M 20 YEARS OLD!! EVERYONE GET REAL EXCITED BECAUSE I WAS BORN...TWENTY YEARS AGO...THIS VERY NIGHT!

Squirrel Girl @unbeatablesg
Fav to wish me happy birthday, RT to wish me an EXTRA happy birthday

Nancy W. @sewwiththeflo
@unbeatablesg Have we worked out the etiquitte of wishing YOURSELF a happy birthday on social media?

Squirrel Girl @unbeatablesg
@sewwiththeflo what if YOU wished me happy birthday, then I could RT that? what if that was a thing we made happen

Nancy W. @sewwiththeflo
Happy birthday to Squirrel Girl, who is both one of my favorite super heroes AND one of my favorite people.

Squirrel Girl @unbeatablesg
@sewwiththeflo aww Nancy!! <3 <3 <3

Tony Stark @starkmantony ✓
@unbeatablesg Are you having a party? Assuming you are having a party, can I come?

Squirrel Girl @unbeatablesg
@starkmantony YES BUT YOU HAVE TO WEAR THE ARMOR

Tony Stark @starkmantony ✓
@unbeatablesg Is this a setup to get me so hepped up on cake that you can convince me to let YOU wear the armor?

Squirrel Girl @unbeatablesg
@starkmantony haha no

Squirrel Girl @unbeatablesg
@starkmantony it's my birthday

Squirrel Girl @unbeatablesg
@starkmantony i'm definitely ending up in that armor tony

Squirrel Girl @unbeatablesg
@starkmantony none can deny me my one true birthday wish

Odinson @num1odinson
@unbeatablesg I pray thee, might Asgardians come to thy party??

Nancy W. @sewwiththeflo
@num1odinson YES BRING LOKI

Odinson @num1odinson
@sewwiththeflo Though I may no longer wield Mjolnir, that does not mean I have been demoted to my brother's secretary service.

Nancy W. @sewwiththeflo
@num1odinson Hmm wow that's a super weird way to spell "yes I will absolutely bring Loki to this party and also Thor, excellent idea Nancy"

Nancy W. @sewwiththeflo
@unbeatablesg I'd be interested in knowing how that little baby born 20 years ago became Squirrel Girl.

Squirrel Girl @unbeatablesg
@sewwiththeflo YES! YES. It is an amazing story.

Nancy W. @sewwiththeflo
@unbeatablesg ...And?

Squirrel Girl @unbeatablesg
@sewwiththeflo And it goes...a little something...A'LIKE THIS.

Nancy W. @sewwiththeflo
@unbeatablesg ...

Nancy W. @sewwiththeflo
@unbeatablesg ...so were you going to post something after that, or

Five Years Later

DING-DONG

Doreen, it's your guests! It's time for your birthday party!

Yay!

Now remember, like we practiced, Doreen. Tail in the pants, we don't wanna give away any secrets.

Tail in the pants! No secrets!!

Hello, Kimberly! Hello, Ashley! Hello, Tyler and Cameron!

Hello Doreen's mom!!

Hey, guys.

Pickup in three hours, right?

You're welcome to stay.

Hah! Dorian, this is our first no-kids afternoon in months. They're alllll yours.

Sure you don't want to stay and--

Too late! I'm alre fantasizing abo quiet restaura with actual cera plates, sorry!

Thank Dor! Y and Maur have f

Where are the crossover restaurants that give you both the classy ambiance and the charmingly snooty maitre d', but *also* the crayons and the paper tablecloth you draw on? "No idea," you whisper, as we both smuggle our crayons and coloring books past the charmingly snooty maitre d'.

THIS JUST IN: Five-year-old Doreen is unbeatably *adorable*, surprising no one.

Geez, it just hit me that the parties we go to as adults *never* have goodie bags that you get to take home at the end! ADULTS, I HAVE SOME BAD NEWS: somewhere along the line, *we totally lost our way.*

ve years later...

It's **not fair**, Foomy. Everyone at school **hates me**. They **literally hate me!**

=sniff=

And I didn't even **do** anything!

They tease me **so much**, and they don't even **know** about my **tail!** They're gonna think I'm an even **bigger** loser if they ever find out!!

"Oooh, Doreen, we're your parents! We're gonna force you to move to a **new town** where you don't know anyone! It **definitely** won't be horrible when you're alone on your birthday because all the stupid kids in this stupid town already hate you!"

Chht chtty chkkk chiiiiiiange eventually, little girl! You won't always be so sad!

What?! Who's spying on me, you--

Ahhh, a **talking squirrel!!**

Ahhh, a **talking human!!**

I am happy to report that close reading of Doreen's Thing clock suggests that it's **always** clobbering time. Please, govern yourselves accordingly.

This squirrel learns he can communicate with a new species for the very first time, and the very first message he transmits is "send more peanut butter." This, sadly, once again confirms that it was actually a good idea to not put squirrels in charge of the messages sent into deep space on the *Voyager* spacecraft.

I can't point you to the precise comic where Captain America saves the moon, but I'm certain there is one. And if there isn't, guess what: *I am so ready to write!*

DID YOU KNOW: This part of Doreen's life was written by Will Murray, who wrote her first appearance back in 1992! But then I added these little notes beneath his pages, because we're pals. Yes. I'm almost *certain* we're pals.

Okay, I'm gonna give Doreen a pass here because she's 15, but for *your* information, the best response to a suspected head injury is "call a doctor," not "say 'Maybe it'll wear off' and then get into a fistfight with a super villain." It's not even in the top *ten* best things to do in response to a head injury!

IN PARTICULAR, HULK DID NOT BECOME GIANT GREEN RAGE MONSTER SO THAT HE COULD WAIT QUIETLY IN LINE AT THE BANK, AND THAT IS ALL HULK WILL SAY ON THE MATTER!!

This illustrates the Hulk's Famous English catchphrase *"Hulk smash,"* which is of course derived From his original Famous Latin catchphrase *"veni, vidi, smashi."*

Dang it I really should've peered through the window before smashing through the wall dang it Red Skull *you know this*

Squirrel Girl did eventually open Loki's present, and once she got rid of the Asgardian Lesser Prank Beast that was making those noises, a lot of the stuff in there was actually really sweet. *The end.*

Twenty-five years ago this month, ~~RVEL~~ SUPER-HEROES WINTER ~~CIAL~~ #8 hit the stands, with stories ~~ring~~ the X-Men, Drax, Gamora, ~~or~~...and a brand new character ~~ed~~ SQUIRREL GIRL!

~~o~~ we're all thrilled and honored to ~~e~~ Doreen's co-creator Will Murray ~~ribute~~ to this anniversary issue by ~~ing~~ that tale of 15-year-old Doreen ~~the~~ Hulk – such a fun story, right? ~~we're~~ paying tribute to SG's other ~~creator~~, the legendary Steve Ditko, ~~unning~~ a panel of his art from that ~~inal~~ story back on the page where ~~ee~~ Doreen's initial costume design! ~~yeah~~, that wasn't actually Doreen's ~~ving~~ – she was a talented artist for ~~-year-old~~, but not THAT talented!)

~~nd~~ TWO years ago this month, THE ~~EATABLE~~ SQUIRREL GIRL #1 (Vol. 1) ~~released~~, so we're celebrating that ~~stone~~ this issue as well! Thanks to ~~ou~~ readers out there for supporting ~~book~~ like crazy, and for sending us ~~letters~~ and your photos and your ~~vings~~ – it's so great knowing these ~~ies~~ are connecting with you! So ~~keep~~ that love coming, and we'll ~~telling~~ more Squirrel Girl stories! ~~boy~~ are there some exciting ones ~~ing~~ up...!)

~~rrel~~ Girl team,

I couldn't believe it when I read the word "zot" in regards to sending items back in time. I am the only person I know who ever uses that word, despite its incredible usefulness. I'm guessing at least one of you played "Story Machine," that old Texas Instrument writing game with that weird purple hand monster.

Best!
Michele

RYAN: No, I've never played it! But there are few phrases more intriguing than "Texas Instrument writing game with that weird purple hand monster", so COLOR ME INTRIGUED. Since we're (tangentally) talking about calculators, let me say that I do all my calculation on an 37-year-old HP 41-CX, an RPN calculator my dad bought before I was born, and of the type that was used on Space Shuttle missions as a backup way to calculate re-entry if the main computer failed. I mostly use it to add up numbers that are too big for me to do in my head.

ERICA: I've never even owned a fancy calculator, seeing as from sixth grade on I attended arts-focused schools. My frame of reference for "Zot" is the Scott McCloud comic, which is great. There's interdimensional travel there! To a futuristic world! That's LIKE time travel, I guess. Also, according to Google, zot is god in Albanian. We learn something new every day.

Ryan and Erica,
I'd never been into reading comics before my husband put your first issue of SQUIRREL GIRL into my hands. I've been hooked from page one when she starts singing her own theme song to the tune of Spider-Man's theme! (Though, admittedly, I had to look up Spider-Man's theme online so I knew the tune because that's how out of touch I started with comics and super heroes...) Still! SQUIRREL GIRL has made me a comics convert thanks to her commitment to kicking butt but also to solving problems with smarts and friendship. She is basically a huge inspiration to anyone who ever wondered if it was possible to eat nuts AND save the world with some smart observations and a few well-placed butt-kicks!

Your delightful comic inspired my own crafts-building as well, and now I have my very own cobbled-together Squirrel Girl doll crew assembled as well as a crocheted Tippy Toe that I used to make a stop motion of the first scene of issue #v1 that drew me into this fabulous squirrelly world so quickly! I attached a few pictures of the dolls I've made (I even have Nancy in anticipation of future films, wearing a shirt that I hope Mew would approve of!) and here's the link to the short stop motion: https://youtu.be/1otZ-PJcCi8

Many thanks for all you do, can't wait for the next nutty adventure!

April Duclos
Massachusetts

about 10 seconds long. ~~Spider-Man~~ said "Time for some heavy reading" and then tried to lift up a newspaper (giant, compared to his action-figure size), and then it collapsed on top of him and he said "Oh no, maybe a little TOO heavy!" I have no regrets.

ERICA: Ryan.

Dear Unbeatable Squirrel Warriors

I just finished 14 and must say, I am impressed with the level of thought that you put into your stories, whether using binary to count on one hand, acting like yelp for Galactus, or physics to defeat Enigmo, Doreen is truly unbeatable. It is great how Doreen and Nancy work so well together!

I have been a longtime fan of SG and am currently working on owning every single one of her appearances, so far I am ten issues away from completion! I am loving every comic you both have put out and know I will continue to enjoy Squirrel Girl's adventures forever!

Ryan, when will we learn more about Nancy? we know so little about her besides she loves Mew, Doreen, knitting, writing Cat-Thor fan fics and maybe has a tattoo?

Erica what has been your favorite panel to draw to date? Is there a character from the Marvel Universe that you would love to draw in a future issue?

P.S. I have enclosed a picture I drew of Doreen and Nancy having a bit of fun!

P.P.S. Just want to finally say that you guys are so lucky working for in my opinion for the best comic company AND the BEST character in the world! keep up the great work Ryan, Erica, Rico, and Travis, I am seriously jealous of all of you!

RYAN: Ah, such a cute drawing!! Besides the fun reveal of FUTURE NANCY in this issue, I also hope we'll be finding out more about Present Nancy soon. Including: NANCY'S

MYSTERIOUS SECRETS??

ERICA: Hm. Last issue I got to draw Taskmaster, who I encouraged Ryan to put in a story because he is a skeleton pirate, so THAT was fun. I don't know about favorite panel, but the part that was the most surprisingly fun to draw was the multiple Squirrel Girls vs Doctor Doom fight, which I thought was just going to be terrible because it was like 20 people per panel.

Dear Squirrel Team,

I just read issue #11 (I know, I'm late, it's embarrassing) and, as a Computer Science student, I couldn't resist sending you my opinion in the form of an algorithm.

```
WHILE (reading){
    I_am_mesmerized();
    IF (Doc Ock appears){
        I_dont_realize_its_weird();
    }
}
I_love_it();
I_think_it_is_perfect();
IF (Someone wants to learn about CS){
    I_give_him_or_her_this_issue();
}ELSE{
    I_force_him_or_her_to_read_it();
}
```

Yours nerdly,
Roni Kaufman

P.S.: I don't know whether I'm the first one to do this. If this not the case, I apologize (another if statement?!).

RYAN: This is great, and I will gladly accept all reader letters in the form of flattering pseudocode from now on!!

ERICA: WHAT IS THIS SORCERY.

Dear Nancy, Doreen, Ryan, and Erica,
I've been a Marvel fan since I was 13 and my daughter Wanda was taught to read with Power Pack comics (POW! BAM! WHAP!). We both absolutely love THE UNBEATABLE SQUIRREL GIRL and giggle maniacally when we read the books again and again. I really like how she solves problems in new and unusual non-violent ways, yet still can appreciate a good butt-kicking occasionally. We enjoyed the Ratatosk storyline so much that we were inspired to do something special this Halloween (see attached pictures). I really hope that Squirrel Girl and Spider-Man can hang out together in the future, and Wanda wants to see more Brain Drain. Thank you so much for all your great work!

Sincerely,
Doug Smith (46) and Wanda Smith (10)

RYAN: Wanda, this part is only [for] **you, so don't let your dad read t**[his:] **that costume is amazing, there**['s] **more Brain Drain in this issue, and** [we] **can retcon that to say it was JUST** [for] **YOU, and thank you so much for be**[ing] **such a great reader! You're the** [best] **Wanda I've ever met AND THEREF**[ORE] **THE BEST.**

Okay Dave, this part of the ans[wer] **is for you: Doreen and Spider-M**[an] **do (briefly) hang out in the SQUIR**[REL] **GIRL BEATS UP THE MARVEL UNIVE**[RSE] **OGN, and it doesn't work out su**[per] **well for... well, the Marvel Univers**[e I] **guess? But I'd like to see more of** [it] **too! She already seems to encou**[nter] **his villains an awful lot. Also,** [tell] **Wanda her costume is awesome!**

ERICA: Brain Drain is so much [fun] **to draw. I second this. Also that is** [an] **amazing Thor outfit. I'm a propon**[ent] **of capes as everyday fall wear so** [my] **choice of the word "outfit" rather t**[han] **"costume" was on purpose.**

Next: New Costume[?]

THE COMPLETE TALE OF THE DARING ADVENTURES OF THE ONE AND ONL[Y] **SQUIRREL GIRL**